ORIGINAL
CORVETTE
1968-1982

Other titles available in the *Original* series are:

Original AC Ace & Cobra
by Rinsey Mills
Original Aston Martin DB4/5/6
by Robert Edwards
Original Austin Seven
by Rinsey Mills
Original Austin-Healey (100 & 3000)
by Anders Ditlev Clausager
Original Citroën DS
by John Reynolds with Jan de Lange
Original Corvette 1953-1962
by Tom Falconer
Original Corvette 1963-1967
by Tom Falconer
Original Ducati Sport & Super Sport 1972-1986
by Ian Falloon
Original Ferrari V8
by Keith Bluemel
Original Ferrari V12 1965-1973
by Keith Bluemel
Original Honda CB750
by John Wyatt
Original Jaguar E-Type
by Philip Porter
Original Jaguar Mark I/II
by Nigel Thorley
Original Jaguar XJ
by Nigel Thorley
Original Jaguar XK
by Philip Porter
Original Land-Rover Series I
by James Taylor
Original Mercedes SL
by Laurence Meredith
Original MG T Series
by Anders Ditlev Clausager

Original MGA
by Anders Ditlev Clausager
Original MGB
by Anders Ditlev Clausager
Original Mini Cooper and Cooper S
by John Parnell
Original Morgan
by John Worrall and Liz Turner
Original Morris Minor
by Ray Newell
Original Pontiac GTO 1964-1974
by Tom de Mauro
Original Porsche 356
by Laurence Meredith
Original Porsche 911
by Peter Morgan
Original Porsche 924/944/968
by Peter Morgan
Original Rolls-Royce & Bentley 1946-65
by James Taylor
Original Sprite & Midget
by Terry Horler
Original Triumph TR2/3/3A
by Bill Piggott
Original Triumph TR4/4A/5/6
by Bill Piggott
Original Triumph Stag
by James Taylor
Original Vincent
by J. P. Bickerstaff
Original VW Beetle
by Laurence Meredith
Original VW Bus
by Laurence Meredith

ORIGINAL
CORVETTE
1968-1982

by Tom Falconer

Photography by James Mann

To my father and mother, Peter and Mary Falconer.

ACKNOWLEDGEMENTS
With many thanks to my wife Polly and children Olivia, Daisy and Alec for their patience, and to James Mann for his excellent photographs.
Special thanks are due to the members of the Mason Dixon Chapter of the National Corvette Restorers Society, particularly Fred Mullauer who found all the
cars and the following who allowed their cars to be photographed and gave freely of their time: Michael Streckfus, Duane Ravenberg, Tony Avidisian,
Andrew Toman, Butch Moxley, Mike Moxley, James Pasko, Herb Abdill, Steve Higginbottom, Lee Sherman, Bill Fink, Jerry Fink, Ray Morrison,
Kim Jordan, Pete Alatzas, Dick Benton, Chuck Berge, Tim Humphreys, Rick Gondeck, Bill Benton, Frank Stech, Bill McVeigh, Pat Gongloff, John Hock,
Ken Brown, Larry Kupka, and their friends. Thanks also to NCRS UK chairman Trevor Rogers for additional photography and support.

I also acknowledge and thank the authors of each of the works in the bibliography; one cannot write a book on
such an already well researched subject without reading and comparing their work first.

Finally thanks to my editor Charles Herridge, who has gently encouraged me to finish this third volume in the series when the daily pressure
of running a Corvette business seems to leave no spare time. I thank you the reader in advance for your comments and corrections, which
should be sent to the author care of the publisher or e-mailed direct to the author, whose e-mail address is tfalconer@btinternet.com

First published in 2001 by MBI Publishing Company,
Galtier Plaza, Suite 200, 380 Jackson Street,
St. Paul, MN 55101-3885 USA

© Tom Falconer 2001

MBI Publishing Company books are also available at
discounts in bulk quantity for industrial or sales-promotional
use. For details write to Special Sales Manager at
Motorbooks International Wholesalers & Distributors,
Galtier Plaza, Suite 200, 380 Jackson Street,
St. Paul, MN 55101-3885 USA.

Library of Congress Cataloging-in-Publication
Data Available

ISBN:0-7603-0897-7

Designed by Chris Fayers, Morwenstow, Cornwall

Printed in China

CONTENTS

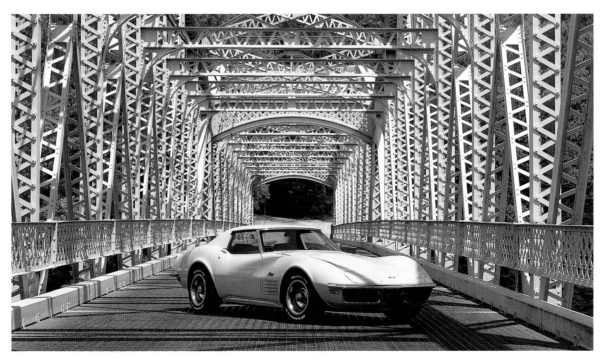

INTRODUCTION

William L. Mitchell had the perfect job. He was chief designer at the world's largest manufacturing corporation and largest car manufacturer. He loved cars and he loved his work. Under his direct control he had hundreds of designers, stylists, sculptors, engineers, artists, model-makers, trimmers and mechanics - indeed he could have built any car that he wanted.

He was expected to lead from the top, and General Motors Corporation expected him to build inspirational dream cars. His predecessor Harley Earl had built the Y-Job and then the fantastic La Salle and used them as his personal cars. Earl saw the Cadillac as the ultimate car, but fortunately for us it was not Cadillacs that Mitchell dreamed of - it was Corvettes.

Appointed Head of Styling in 1958 he quickly found the chassis from the 1957 SS 'mule', the spare car that had been taken to Sebring along with the SS for GM's brief foray into sports car racing, which had immediately been terminated by worried senior management. Together with stylist Larry Shinoda, Mitchell built his own sports-racing car on this chassis and called it the Sting Ray.

He may have been indulging his hobby, but this one project was of inestimable benefit to the future of the Corvette, because the car was raced successfully from April 1959, gave Dick Thompson a class win in the 1960 SCCA championship, and then became the prototype for the 1963 Corvette Sting Ray. Once this was in production Mitchell needed a new project. There were other proposals for the next generation of Corvette, but he knew exactly what he wanted.

Still with an eye on the racetrack (the one with corners not the drag strip) Bill Mitchell's endless enthusiasm started him on his next ultimate personal car. This was to be the Mako Shark II, the uncompromized and perfect form which would ultimately become the prototype for the 1968 Stingray. It was a design dominated by its wheels - radical 7½in wide rims wearing 8.80 front and 10.30 rear racing tires, with the wheel housings massively accentuated and sculpted into a mean and selfish passenger compartment. The 1963 Corvette had cleverly accommodated the necessary wheels into a pure form and given them a balanced presence in the overall design. Now for the Mako Shark II the wheels were made absolutely dominant. No production road tires were available in the size required for this prototype, this dream car for the future, but Mitchell knew that they were coming even if he had to design them for Goodyear himself.

The Mako Shark II debuted as a non-running mock-up, built on a 1965 Sting Ray chassis, and was initially shown to an amazed public at the New York International Motor Show in April 1965. It had finned twin outside exhaust headers leading into matching side-pipes, with the edges of the fins polished. The hood was a forward-tilting clam shell, the windshield wipers were completely hidden under a retracting panel, the roof was hinged at the B pillars, power lifted when the doors opened, the louvers over the tapered back window rotated when rear vision was required, and there were retracting rear bumpers and spoiler too. Inside there was an airplane style butterfly steering wheel, electrically powered pedals instead of adjustable seats, and digital instrumentation which would become reality on Corvettes 18 years ahead. At the touch of a button even the rear number plate could be rotated, and not just to keep it clean!

Immediately after the New York show, the car was turned into a fully running and driveable road car. A 427 V8 big-block and Turbo Hydra-Matic automatic transmission were installed, the outside exhausts were changed for an under-car system with massive rectangular rear outlets, and a round two-spoke steering wheel was substituted for the butterfly item. Now the car embarked on a world tour starting with the Paris Salon in October and followed by the London Earls Court Motor Show, where it made such an impression that all 1968-82 Corvettes are still referred to as Mako Sharks by British enthusiasts, even 35 years later! A tour of the world's motor shows followed, with Mitchell often in attendance to demonstrate his dream car, including (he claimed when I interviewed him in London in 1984) pacing the Monaco Grand Prix in Monte Carlo.

Bill Mitchell first worked as a stylist for General Motors under Harley Earl in 1935, spent the war with the US Navy, rejoined GM in 1954 and became Vice President, Styling, in 1958. He retired in 1977 and died on September 12 1988. He never designed for Board approval, loved upsetting his fellow directors, was a true car fanatic and created automobiles for his fellow car enthusiasts. He was responsible for the styling of an incredible 78 million cars, but his greatest legacy is the two generations of Corvettes built from 1963 to 1982.

CORVETTE BASICS

NAMES

The Corvette has been built by Chevrolet, a division of General Motors Corporation, since 1953. In 1962, the all-new 1963 model Corvette was given the additional name Sting Ray. This continued to be used until the model was replaced by the 1968 Corvette, which had no additional name. In 1969 the name Stingray, one word, was added and then dropped again for 1977. By this time the 1963-67 cars were often being called Mid-year Corvettes. When Chevrolet were developing the new-shaped 1997 Corvette they gave it the code name C5, short for Corvette Five, because it would be the fifth generation. So not only are 1963-67 Corvettes called Sting Rays and Mid-Years but now C2s as well.

The 1968-82 models covered in this book cannot all be called Stingrays because the word was not used in 1968 advertising, nor was the emblem fitted to the car. For the 1977 model year the use of Stingray abruptly ceased and the name has not been seen on a Chevrolet since. It is no coincidence that this was when the great Bill Mitchell, Head of Styling, finally left: it was he who loved sea fishing and thought that his favorite model deserved a piscatorial name. He chose the name originally, applying it first to his own successful 1959 Corvette Sting Ray racer. This car used his own design of body and this was grafted onto the abandoned Corvette SS Mule, whose only outing had been practise at Sebring in 1957.

1968-72 Corvettes are often called Chrome Bumpers, and more recently Shark has been applied to these models or even the whole 1968-82 series, something that would certainly have pleased Mitchell. The back window design of the 1968-77 coupes is often called the sugar scoop, while all 1968-82s are correctly C3s.

MODEL YEARS

The model year was and still is three to four months in advance of the calendar year, so the 1968 model year ran from September 1967 to August 1968. This system, which began in the mid-1950s, allowed for summer vacations and re-tooling for the model changeover. Exceptionally, because of a labor strike in May 1969, model changeover to the 1970 model was delayed until January 1970. Minor changes were introduced each September, to ensure that the new model looked new. Unlike European practise, an American car cannot be passed off as newer by delaying its date of first registration.

VIN NUMBERS

The most important number on the car was the vehicle identification number, VIN, which was

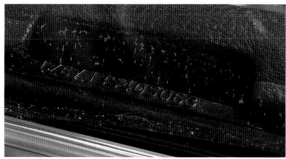

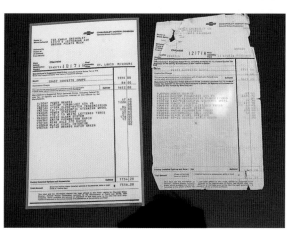

The all-important VIN (vehicle identification number), is found on the driver's side windshield pillar on all 1968 to 1982 Corvettes. This is a 1970.

Window sticker showed the ordering dealer, the options and their prices and the final cost of the car. An original is a prized document because most were torn off and discarded.

reverse stamped on a plate riveted to the bottom front face of the driver's windshield pillar and visible only through the glass. This was the permanent number which related to the Corvette's title and registration. To help prevent fraud the windshield would have to be removed to tamper with the VIN plate, which was also secured with unique 'rose' headed rivets.

For 1968-80 the VIN was a 13-character number. The VIN incorporated the Division code, car series and body style, and assembly plant, in front of the sequential serial number. The first 1969 coupe built was 194379S100001, if it was a coupe, which breaks down as follows:

1	Chevrolet Division of General Motors.
94	Corvette Series. An even second number, here a 4, indicates a V8 engine.
37	2-door coupe. 67 would be a convertible.
9	model year 1969
S	built at St Louis, Missouri, assembly plant.
100001	sequential number

The final 1971 built was sequential number 121801, which was the 21,801st car built, referred to in the text for simplicity as car 21,801.

In 1972 a new 13-character VIN series was introduced, which would run through 1980. The car series was now denoted by a single letter, instead of a pair of numbers, making space for an engine identification letter. So the first 1972 built, if it was a coupe and fitted with the base small block engine, was VIN 1Z37K2S500001, which breaks down as follows:

1	Chevrolet Division of General Motors.
Z	Corvette Series.
37	2 -door coupe. 67 would be a convertible.
K	350 200hp (L was the 350 255hp and W the 454 270hp)
2	model year 1972
S	built at St Louis, Missouri, assembly plant
500001	sequential number

The final 1977 built was sequential number 449213, which was the 49,213rd car built, referred to in the text for simplicity as car 49,213.

Engine fifth character codes for Corvettes from 1972 to 1980 are:

H	1980 305 California LG4
J	1973-75 350 Base
K	1972 350 Base
L	1972 350 LT1
L	1976-78 350 L48
L	1980 350 L82
T	1973-75 350 L82
W	1972 454
X	1976-77 350 L82
Z	1973-74 454
4	1978-79 350 L82
8	1979-80 350 L48

In 1981 the system changed yet again to the 17 character system still in use in 2001. So the first 1981 built, a coupe fitted with the only engine available was VIN IG1AY8764BS400001, which breaks down as follows:

1	assembled in the United States
G	General Motors
1	Chevrolet Division of General Motors
AY	Corvette
87	2-door coupe
6	engine code, 190hp L81 V8, 1982 L83 was an 8
4	check code
B	model year 1981, C was 1982 etc
S	built at St Louis, Missouri assembly plant
400001	sequential number

On June 1st 1981, Corvette assembly started at the new Bowling Green plant whose plant code was 5 and the sequential number started afresh at 100001.

6	1981 350 L81
8	1982 350 L83

ENGINE CODES

All Corvette 327 and 350 small-block engines fitted to Corvettes were assembled at Flint, Michigan. As the engine was assembled it was stamped with a code identifying the plant, date and limited specification of the engine. An engine assembled for a 1969 Corvette with the L46 350hp 350cu in engine, air conditioning and manual transmission built on February 17 1969 would be stamped V0217HX in ³⁄₁₆in high letters on the right-hand side of the block code pad in front of the right-hand cylinder head.

In this example:

V	Flint engine assembly plant
02	February
17	17th day of the month
HX	L46 engine fitted with air-conditioning pulleys and a flywheel, not a flex plate. In 1970, the suffix became three letters starting with C/, which probably denoted car because truck engines for this period used a T. Engine two- and three-letter suffix codes are listed at the end of each chapter. Big-block engines all came from Tono-wanda, so the first V became a T.

When the engine reached St Louis, a further stamping was made onto the left side of the pad, which was known as a VIN derivative, in letters ⅛in high. This started with a 1 denoting Chevrolet, followed the last numeral of the model year, then the assembly plant code, which was S for St Louis, then the full sequential number. For example the first 1969 Corvette would be stamped at the left of the pad 9S100001, where 9 is the model year and 100001 the number that follows the S plant code in the VIN number.

TRIM TAG

This was a stainless steel plate located on the steel body birdcage reinforcement, directly above the driver's upper door hinge, held in position with two pop rivets. It revealed much important information, including the build date of the body and the original interior and exterior colors. The top line read CHEVROLET followed by a month code and the day that the body was built.

The 1968-77 code used letters to indicate the month, starting with A as August. There were exceptions because of strikes, for 1970 when it

Door sticker showed the VIN, month and year of build and weight ratings as required by the government. This is from a 1972, the first year to show an engine code. W indicates a 270hp 454.

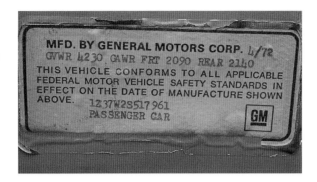

1982 door stickers.

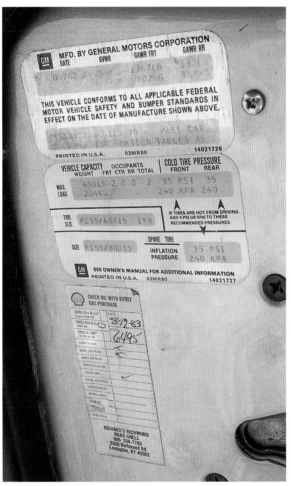

stood for January 1970, and 1975, when A represented the late start to production in October 1974 . The numbers 1 to 31 indicated the day date. For 1965 model year, A was August 1964 and L July 1965. For 1966 and 1967, the pattern was the same with A as August, except that for St Louis built bodies in 1966 A was September.

The next line indicated the numerical trim code after the word TRIM. In 1968 and 1969 only the letters STD indicate a black vinyl interior, for 1975 and 1976 the letter suffix V indicated vinyl. and for 1977 C indicated the optional cloth center panels to the seats. The external color code, as listed at the end of each chapter, was then shown before the word PAINT.

MATCHING NUMBERS

This term is much used and misused. As a minimum, a 'matching numbers' car to most enthusiasts means that the stampings on the front of the engine are correct and original and that they match the information on the VIN tag on the left-hand windshield pillar. More generously it means that every component that carries a VIN derivative number, particularly the frame and transmission, have been checked and match. 'All matching numbers' or 'Full matching numbers' really means that every component that carries a checkable cast or stamped number is correct. This implies that the dates of all components precede the build date on the trim tag by a reasonable time.

The majority of 1968-77 Corvettes are almost full matching numbers and it is fun to check a car to confirm this. Among the most likely incorrect parts will be the alternator and water pump, items that are normally replaced in service with reconditioned units. Big-block cars are less likely to have their original engines than small-blocks because they have often been driven harder and sustain abuse less readily than small-blocks.

Sadly, there will always be those who will pass off a fake as the genuine article, and it is possible to

Right: The body trim plate showed day and month of final assembly, paint color code, and interior trim material and color. This is a 1970 plate. Far right: A 1982 body trim plate.

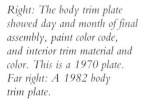

fake any engine only too easily. If you over-rev your 427 435 L71 1969 big-block, and a connecting rod punctures the cylinder block, you are facing not only a large repair bill but also a much larger permanent reduction in the value of your car, as much as half. It is easy, but completely fraudulent, to deck another block, re-stamp it and present it as original. For this reason the engine casting number, described below, is at least as important as the stamped numbers, because it is harder, though not impossible, to fake.

PART NUMBERS & CAST NUMBERS

In any publication with the word 'Original' in its title, manufacturers' part numbers are going to be important. As the world's largest maker of road vehicles, it is to be expected that General Motors' parts system should be pretty well organized and it is. Part numbers were assigned by Chevrolet to every part as the car was designed, and incorporated into the Assembly Instruction Manual and Chevrolet Parts and Illustration Catalogs even before the first cars were sold. While parts were sent to St Louis to be incorporated into new cars, more were boxed for service and repair, to be sold by General Motors Parts Division. A division of GM in its own right, it publishes parts catalogs, at one time only on paper, now only as fiche or on disk. It also warehouses and distributes the parts to GM dealers.

Parts are all considered to be GM and are not identified in their labeling or boxing as belonging to the different car divisions, because so many are common to some or all of them. Only by reference to the application codes in the GM Dealers Parts and Accessories Price Schedule is it possible to identify which divisions use a certain part number. If the supplier of a part, the original equipment manufacturer, is changed, or if it is improved in some way, then the part number will be changed too.

Cast iron parts will have a part number, which will appear on the box if it is correctly boxed, but which will not be marked on the part. The important number is the cast number, which will be visible if indistinct through corrosion, and will be different to the part number in the catalog or Assembly Instruction Manual. There should also be a cast date.

The part number will be found in an old parts book or in the Assembly Instruction Manual, but not on the part. Unfortunately, probably less than five per cent of all the parts listed in the parts book for the 1968-82 are still available from General Motors, so the part numbers are interesting, but not a lot of use to the restorer.

The cast numbers are much more useful, which is why they are mentioned so often in this book. They can prove whether a part is original and correct or

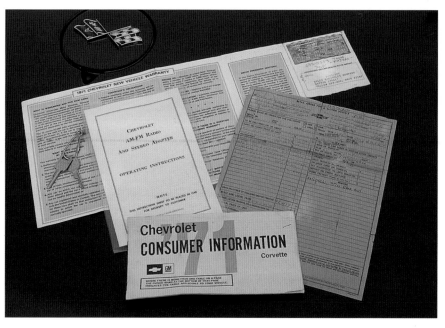

not. Consider a 1968 300hp 327cu in base option cylinder head. It had the number 3917291 cast in the valve chest. In this engine it had 1.94in intake valves, but the same head was also machined for 2.02in intake valves for the 1968 350hp 327engines. When a casting was machined in two different ways then each part was normally assigned a different part number. These heads were also used on hundreds of thousands of full-size Chevrolets, Camaros, Chevelles and even Chevy IIs too, which makes them easy to find. All small-block cylinder heads are interchangeable side for side, but many parts such as exhaust manifolds are handed left or right.

While cast numbers are not part numbers, they adhere to the same convention - odd numbers left and even numbers right. The very few exceptions to this rule are usually caused by the application of a popular part in a different handed way, such as 1968 and later Corvette electric window motors. The Corvette is a left hand drive car and left-hand parts are those on the driver's side. Parts not fitted to a car in pairs can have part numbers that are odd or even. This odd and even parts number convention is extremely useful when sorting through used parts at a swap meet or when checking GM boxed parts. Surprisingly, many experienced Chevrolet countermen are unaware of it. Even some of the major aftermarket Corvette parts specialists, who re-number all parts to their own codes, ignore this very sensible convention. A very large number of wrongly supplied parts are simply the right part in the wrong hand, and GM probably adopted this system to avoid this. Sadly, since the mid-1990s General Motors themselves have lost their way on this and a significant number of C4 and later parts are now 'wrongly' numbered.

Next to the casting number there is usually a date code. General Motors and their many suppliers used

An original dealer's invoice, usually written by hand but sometimes with a typewriter, is a most desirable document from the pre-computer era.

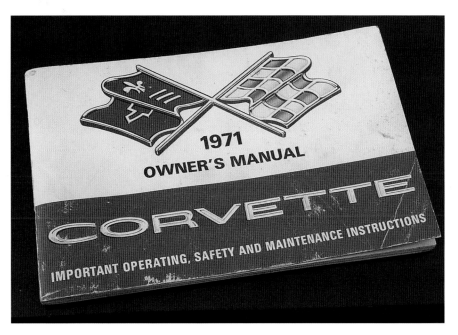

The original Owner's Manual came with a tear-out card offering a free subscription to Chevrolet's fascinating Corvette News. Manuals are now available in reproduction

hidden when installed. Often the date is also obscured by the steel splash shield which is riveted below the carburetor.

Many parts, such as carburetors, had a number stamped into them, and this is referred to as the stamped number. It was more likely to correspond to the original part number. AC Delco distributors usually had an aluminum band, stamped with the part number and date, wrapped around the base just above the clamp. These bands can be bought easily so they prove nothing about the distributor's provenance unless supported by other evidence.

Unfortunately, cast numbers too can be faked, and in the case of expensive, rare and desirable Corvettes it is important to check with more books than this one, consult with your local NCRS chapter, and best of all trace and talk with previous owners.

this system to expedite quality control. If a casting flaw was found, the whole batch could be pulled out of the system before they reached the customer. Heavy castings such a cylinder heads, manifolds and blocks were cast at Flint, north of Detroit, Michigan, and at Tonawanda, near Niagara Falls, New York. Because the Corvette was assembled in St Louis, just across the Mississippi, small-block engines were cast, machined and built at Flint, which was much closer geographically than Tonowanda. Flint castings generally have a single numeral to represent the year element of the date code, while Tonowanda used two. So in 1969 Flint castings would have carried the year code 9, while Tonowanda would use 69. The year was preceded by the month and day, with the months January to December using the letters A to L. So a cylinder head with cast date code D-12-4 would have been cast on April 12 1969 at Flint. If this was found on an engine whose build date was in March 1969 it would be incorrect or a replacement. Indeed, there would normally be a delay of a week to six months before the head was incorporated into the engine. The date code was adjusted and screwed into the casting machinery every day, and the reverse image of the two screws is usually visible on either side of the code. On small-block engines the date code is generally on the top of the rear flange of the engine, while on big-blocks it is generally on the side of the motor behind the right-hand exhaust manifold.

An aluminum part such as a transmission case or intake manifold would also have a cast number and date. The manifolds of the higher-performance engines fitted to Corvettes were all aluminum and generally cast by the Winters foundry, with their trademark 'snowflake' logo, in Canton, Ohio. They showed their cast number on the top, and date information under the manifold so that it was

OPTIONS

In 1956, the fourth year of Corvette production, the option list became truly optional and the list grew year by year. The point where it was theoretically possible that no two Corvettes would be built alike was passed long since and by 1968 there were 35 options to choose from. The list would eventually peak at 40, not including colors, in 1969.

By making the good stuff optional, Chevrolet could keep the advertised price low. A $21 discount could put you into a stripped three-speed '68 convertible for an enticing $4299, but the option list had become a cult. You proved your performance-car credentials when you checked the right boxes after hours of technical discussion at work and paid the deposit on your new car, and the dealer encouraged you all the way up to and beyond $6600. The choice of options determines the 'character' of a Corvette and is very important in considering a particular car. Generally speaking, you will discover that whatever year of 1968-82 Corvette you own, you will never see an identical one.

The coding of options was refined during the early '60s so that the first letter defined the group of options: A is for body options such as tinted glass, headrests and seatbelts, C for rear window defrosters and air conditioning, L for optional engines and M for transmission options.

These were known as RPO for Regular Production Option codes. There were exceptions such as the PT6 red stripe tires or the UA6 alarm. For readability, the RPO prefix is generally omitted and they are referred to as options. Almost all Corvettes were built to customer order, and only early in the model year would dealers buy cars for stock. So the popularity of options exactly reflects contemporary taste. Option lists were slowly cut back from 1969 on.

1968

Thirty-three years after its September 1967 launch the 1968 Corvette is still one of the most sensational shapes ever devised for a production car. It was a triumph for Bill Mitchell's GM Styling Staff which was at that time probably the largest automotive design facility in the world. One man in particular who deserved credit was Larry Shinoda, who had been involved with Mitchell's Corvette projects since the days of the Sting Ray Racer and was largely responsible for the '63-'67 Corvette styling too.

Bill Mitchell had joined Harley Earl's GM styling team back in 1936, when it was known as 'Art and Colour', complete with pretentious English 'u', and was a master at identifying and understanding trends in automobile development. At the beginning of the 1960s new tires had started to become available after a long period with no changes. Indeed the tires on a 1933 Chevrolet were effectively interchangeable with those on a 1963. Study pictures of the Indy 500, any Grand Prix or Le Mans from 1960 to 1964, and the change from tall to wide tires is striking. The two great sports car designs of this era

were the 1961 Jaguar XKE and the 1963 Sting Ray. Both were beautiful shapes which cleverly accommodated four wheels with the tall tires then available. The genius of the 1968 Corvette designers was that they were the first to grab the sensual appeal of four fat tyres and then emphasize them as never before, with a taut skin that still drew the eye back to the wheels

BODY & BODY TRIM

The 1968 Corvette had certain specific features which distinguish it from the later cars. First it must be made clear that the '68, unlike the 1969-76 models, was never a Stingray. Its front fenders were bare of emblems - the car was just a Corvette. Bill Mitchell loved the romance of deep sea fishing, admired the power and shape of the sharks and rays and projected their color and shapes into many of his designs. He rightly appreciated that at high speed the flow of air over a car is similar to that of fish travelling through water. Somehow the Stingray name got left off for

September 1967 was the launch month for the 1968 Corvette. This very early convertible is finished in Safari Yellow.

DIMENSIONS & WEIGHTS	
Length	182.5in
Width	69.2in
Height	
Sport Coupe	47.75in
Convertible	47.8in
Wheelbase	98.0in
Max track	
Front	58.25in
Rear	59.0in
Curb weight	
Sport Coupe	3210lb
Convertible	3220lb

The removable hardtop (above) was ordered by about half of convertible buyers, its taut shape and concave back window emphasizing the muscular curves of the fiberglass body. As with the superseded 1967 Sting Ray, the coupe version of the Corvette (right) accounted for only a third of production in 1968. The new body was pinched in around the doors (below), earning it the Coke Bottle nickname and restricting cockpit space. But it was worth it!

1968, and it was surely Mitchell's will that put it back on, as one word, in 1969.

The targa, or more popularly t-roof, coupe was a first for Chevrolet. The removable roof panels and back window gave all the fresh air and freedom of the convertible with the roll-over protection of the coupe. The t-roof panels were stored in vinyl bags and stowed safely in the rear compartment with straps provided. The rear window fitted beneath the rear deck in its own swing-down compartment.

The convertible had established itself as a better seller than the coupe by almost two to one over the previous five years of the Sting Ray era and the trend continued for 1968, helped perhaps by a $343 price advantage to the convertible. This car was disappointingly rich in rattles and shakes, though at least with the top down these all seemed to disappear. The removable hardtop, available as a no-cost alternative to the soft top or as an extra to it for an additional $231.75, restored the rattles with a vengeance. The 1968 hardtop was the only one which never had protective points at its extreme rear corners. It could be ordered with a black vinyl covering for extra cost.

Perhaps due to lack of development time, the streamlined external door handles needed an extra button as a thumb push, which also made the door unique because of the button mounted in a recessed aperture in the fiberglass. The driver's door mirror was relocated further back on the door in March 1968, early cars having the mirror fixed almost in line with the A-pillar. Compared to the 1963-67 Sting Ray the 1968 door hinges demonstrate the quality problem that afflicted the new model. The '63-'67 had heavy cast hinges that look like they came off an industrial furnace. I have four new-old-stock ones which I will never be able sell because they never wear out! By contrast the 1968 hinges were stamped out of ⅛in steel with pressed-in bronze bushes and a bent wire locating spring.

The NCRS have identified three different sized headlamp doors for this year, each one ⅛in larger than the previous. Many '68s were dismantled when they were next to worthless, so now we know why we had such problems fitting those early

The front bumper (above) was the thinnest ever on an American car. Only 1968 and early 1969 grilles had the silver painted front edges. On 1968 models only a push button opened the door (left) and the chrome-plated flap dropped to make a finger pull.

COLORS

Code	Quantity	Body	Suggested interior trim
900	708	Tuxedo Black	Black, Dark Blue, Dark Orange, Gunmetal, Medium Blue, Red, Tobacco
972	1868	Polar White	Black, Dark Blue, Dark Orange, Gunmetal, Medium Blue, Red, Tobacco
974	2918	Rally Red	Black, Red,
976	4772	Le Mans Blue	Black, Medium Blue, Dark Blue
978	2473	International Blue	Black, Dark Blue, Medium Blue
983	4779	British Green	Black
984	3133	Safari Yellow	Black
986	3435	Silverstone Silver	Black, Dark Blue, Gunmetal
988	1155	Cordovan Maroon	Black
992	3374	Corvette Bronze	Black, Dark Orange, Tobacco

All wheels were Argent Silver. Convertible top choice was Black, White or Beige.

The driver's door mirror was mounted next to the windshield frame until March 1968, when it was moved back for a better view.

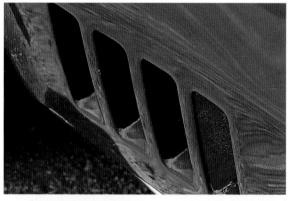

British Green was the most popular color for 1968 (above), closely followed by Le Mans Blue. Only three of the four front fender vents (right) were open. 1968 Corvettes carried no fender emblems.

Black vinyl covering was an optional alternative finish for the hardtop, which was otherwise painted to match the body color. 1969 to 1975 hardtops had protective metal trims on these rear points.

lids into later cars for crash repairs! On 1968 cars only, the windshield washer nozzles are thin tubes which point out from the grille in front of the wiper flap.

CHASSIS

Designed in the early 1960s, this frame had already been proved with five years service in the Sting Ray since 1963. It was a ladder design which allowed the floor pan to be dropped down where appropriate to improve the interior space and the driving position, and swept up at the rear for the all-important independent rear suspension.

This frame remained in production almost unchanged for an amazing 20 years, and it is remarkable that it should have been so right from the outset. It was formed of pairs of pressed U-sections, welded together at intervals and dipped in a cheap black paint. If Corvette owners today could change one aspect of 1963-82 production, zinc plating the frames would be near the top of everyone's list.

The frames were made by A.O. Smith in Granite City, Illinois, close by the St Louis assembly plant. The 1968 frame carried a white stencilled GM part number, appearing upside down at the rear of the right side main rail, followed by A.O. Smith's own lot control and the date. In mid-1968 production was moved back to the A.O. Smith plant in Milwaukee, where the frames had been made prior to 1963.

On the assembly line the frame was stamped with the sequential part of the car's VIN on the top of the left main side rail beneath the door, and again on the top of the left rear rail behind the wheel. The first cannot be read without removing the body, the second can sometimes be seen with a small mirror and a flashlight. Although this number constitutes one of the three principal elements of the concept of 'matching numbers' - engine to body to frame - it cannot be examined readily so is usually ignored even by NCRS judges, who must look for other clues to originality.

The 1968 and later frames featured a fixed transmission crossmember for the manual gearbox but this was removable for the large Turbo Hydra-Matic. It was the last frame to be built without diagonal braces from the kick-up to the axle crossmember

INTERIOR

The exterior of the new Corvette was stunning, but the steeply raked windshield, low roof, sloped door glass and pinched coke-bottle waistline all meant that the interior was going to be tight. No problem with that in a sports car perhaps, but the seat had to be raked back further than in the previous model, 33 degrees instead of 25, and shoulder room was tight.

Molded vinyl with injected polyurethane foam was introduced for Corvette door panels in 1965 and this technology was adopted world wide by General Motors to produce attractive and cheap interior panels. The 1968 Corvette was being developed at the height of this enthusiasm, and so almost every possible interior surface was designed with this material in mind. That was fine for the first owner, but in the long term this material did not wear at all well. In particular the door panels, which were molded onto a pressed fiber base, deteriorated badly from the water which runs down through any door. The early 1968 door panel was particularly unsatisfactory, with no proper internal door pull, only a horizontal hand slot which soon fell apart. This was corrected with a separate horizontal handle in the spring of 1968.

The standard seats were finished in a coarse 'Basket weave' vinyl. They used a cranked pivot to fold forward for access into the rear compartment. The seat back latches were on the left side of each seat, and until late in 1968 production these were mounted very low, to be raised for easier access for the last few thousand cars of the year. Leather was an option and a was stitched in the same pattern as the vinyl. The carpet was loop pile, with vinyl or leather trimming.

Targa roofs (above) were a Corvette first, widely copied. The freedom they offered far outweighed the occasional creaks and leaks. Combined with the removable back window they offered convertible fresh air with full rollover protection. Frameless glass was located and adjusted from within the door (left). It becomes hard to adjust as components wear. The 1968 dash and console (below) were pulled well back because of the more steeply raked windscreen.

The interior was not spacious (right) and the only luggage space was behind the seats. Interior lights (below) mounted on the B-pillars were unique to 1968.

The passenger had no glove box (right) as in the previous five years.

Medium Blue leather interior (below) was a Corvette classic. Like so many, this owner has replaced his 16in steering wheel with a black-rimmed 15in wheel from a 1969-75. Only the 1968 had a dash-mounted ignition switch. The pedal rubbers were neatly trimmed in stainless steel.

The choice of interior colors for 1968 was outstanding, and in the best of the advertising material at the time a beautiful Le Mans blue/ medium blue car was featured against an orange sunset – it was completely beguiling.

INSTRUMENTS & CONTROLS

The new 1968 Federal Motor Vehicle Safety Standards had a major influence on the instruments and interior layout of the 1968 Corvette. The previous 1963-67 generation cars had a magnificent diecast six-gauge cluster directly in front of the driver, and a big clock in the center console. It was easy to read and looked great, but it was too reflective and was damaging in the event of a crash. Now the large 160mph speedo and 7000rpm tachometer, with black faces and green graphics, were recessed deep into a sculpted panel of vinyl faced, impact absorbing polyurethane foam. The five-dial centre cluster incorporated the usual fuel level, ammeter, coolant temperature and oil pressure gauges together with a small clock, all angled towards the driver.

Option U15 was a speedometer with speed warning indicator. When the needle reached the selected position of the adjustable hand, a buzzer sounded but in practice it was hard to hear the buzzer at high speed. Today such buzzers are a legal requirement in some Middle East countries, where they are not at all popular.

The tachometer was supplied with different yellow and red zones for each engine option. The yellow zone indicated the valve float area, while red was the danger zone, always finishing at 7000rpm. On the base 300hp engine the yellow zone spanned 5000-5300rpm and the red zone 5300-7000rpm. On the 350hp the yellow zone was from 5700 to 6000rpm, while for the 390hp and 400hp big-blocks the yellow was from 5300 to 5600rpm, and for the 435hp from 6300 to 6500rpm. In practice no modern owner should go any where remotely close to these yellow zones because of the risk of serious damage to his engine. Thirty years experience has also taught that 4000rpm should be the absolute limit for big-blocks, but more on that below.

The ignition switch position at the top right-hand of the dash beside the tachometer was unique to the 1968. The ammeter, fuel and water temperature gauges were generally accurate in use, while the oil pressure gauge suffered from premature and messy breakage of its plastic hose or failure to indicate pressure at all due to blockage with old oil. The clock used an impulse wound clockwork mechanism made by Borg. The owner's handbook recommended cleaning and oiling periodically, but while it ran no-one bothered, and when it stopped it was too late. Fortunately, reliable quartz or original-type replacement mechanisms are now available to restore failed clocks.

A seat belt warning light on the left side of the center console lit up each time the ignition was switched on and required a push of the square button below it to extinguish it. The right-hand warning lights originally contained a low fuel warning, which was replaced by a door ajar message in the spring of 1968, and a wiper door warning in the lower position.

The major control of any car is the steering wheel and the big 16in fake wood wheel of the 1968 was very similar to, though not interchangeable with, the previous four years' wheel. An optional telescopic column, selected by less than a quarter of buyers, enabled the steering wheel to be adjusted from the standard position, which was really too close to the chest, particularly for shorter drivers.

After years of reliable mechanical linkage, a cable now connected the accelerator pedal to the carburetor. This was prone to stretch and a led to a consequent and sometimes inexplicable loss of top end performance. The wide choice of carburetors for the year, however, made this a sensible move. Mechanical linkage continued to be used for the clutch, but without the reversible link which achieved the adjustable throw offered during the Sting Ray era. The essential adjustment of clutch free play, by a pair of jam nuts, was still easily accessible beside the brake master cylinder under the hood. All pedals carried stylish stainless steel trims.

The parking brake lever was between the seats, where it had moved for the 1967 model. The console now included receiving slots for the seat belt buckles, unique to the year, and the power window switches, when fitted.

ENGINES

There were just two small-block engines offered for 1968, both 5.4-liter 327s: the base 327 300hp and the optional high performance L79 327 350hp. By contrast there were no less than five optional 427 (7-liter) big-blocks, the latter accounting for almost half of total Corvette sales in 1968. As in 1967, small-blocks were designated Turbo Fire and big-blocks Turbo Jet. The misuse of the word 'turbo' is strange, particularly as Chevrolet were offering a real turbocharger as an option on their otherwise normally aspirated Turbo-Air aircooled flat-six Corvair. Similarly in 1962 and '63, sister Division Oldsmobile had turbocharged versions of its 215cu in aluminum motor.

Nominally a carryover from 1967, the 1968 327 shared almost no part numbers with its predecessor - indeed the crankshaft was unique to the Corvette in 1968 and will interchange with no other model year.

The big speedometer and tachometer were each buried down their tunnels. The effect was impressive at night.

This has meant that a correct 1968 Corvette small-block is a tough engine for the restorer to find.

The 1968 327 was a transitional engine, caught on the cusp between the rev hungry 327, whose architecture dated back to the 1955 265 (4.3-liter), and the emissions-ready 350 (5.7-liter), which would power the Corvette through the mid-1990s. The quick way to tell apart a 327 from a 350 is this: 327s had solid valve covers, an oil filler pipe that fitted into the front half of the intake manifold, and most importantly a crankcase vent at the back of the block just beside the distributor. Valve covers and intake manifolds could be changed, but there was no question about that rear block vent. For the 350, Chevrolet decided to sacrifice appearance for efficiency and some cost savings and arranged for all crankcase ventilation and oil filling to be via the valve covers. Armed with this knowledge a trip around a historic car race meeting paddock becomes particularly interesting. Just spot all those modern 350s masquerading as pre-'66 327s...

The 1968 327 was transitional because while it had the crankcase ventilation via the valve covers in the style of the new-generation 350, the oil filler was still in the front of the intake manifold.

Base 327 300hp Looking at the base 300 hp engine in detail, the air cleaner was the classic 14in diameter, 3in deep open-element unit first used on the 1965 396 big-block, and then used generally on all single-carburetor Corvettes for the next five years.

The four-barrel carburetor was a Rochester, for the first time on a Corvette. After two years with Holley as the sole supplier, Rochester, a GM subsidiary, became the main source for the Corvette. The Holley 4150 carburetor had been first used on the Corvette in 1964 on the 365hp 327, and Holley then displaced old reliable Carter to become the sole supplier for all 1966 and 1967 Corvettes. Essentially a race carburetor, the Holley 4150 was easy to work on but not sufficiently sophisticated to handle the upcoming emissions requirements of the late 1960s.

Holleys also tended to be troublesome when hot. The under-hood temperature was increasing year by year, two contributory factors being the universal use of AIR pumps on Corvettes in 1968, which heated up the exhaust manifolds, and the ever increasing popularity of air conditioning. The main weakness of the Holley for road cars was also its strength at the race track. It was partly of vertically split construction, the jet blocks being sandwiched between the float bowls and the main body, sealed with gaskets and attached to either end of the main body. This construction enabled the tuner to change the jets or complete metering block in less than a minute at the race track, but the vertical seals were very prone to leaks, of both gasoline and air.

Maligned as it was, the Rochester Quadrajet four-barrel had much to recommend it. The carburetor was split horizontally, and the all important float bowl would retain its fuel even with no gasket, though occasionally one was found with a porous casting. The principle advantage of the Rochester was its unequal or 'spread' bore. While the Holley had two pairs of $1\frac{11}{16}$in bores, the GM product had $1\frac{3}{8}$in diameter primaries for good mixture speed at low revs, and a pair of massive $2\frac{1}{4}$in secondaries for maximum flow at high speed. The Rochester was rated as having an air flow rate of 700cfm at wide-open throttle. General Motors engineers were no doubt behind the move to 'spread bore' carburetors and intake manifolds, and General Motors accountants were no doubt in favour of in-house sourcing too.

The Quadrajet used from 1968 to 1974 was the model MV4. This unit used a bi-metallic coil in a heat stove on the right-hand side of the intake manifold to operate the choke by a rod, and was actuated by hot exhaust gases passing through the exhaust cross-over passage cast into the intake manifold. To keep the gasoline supply cool and clean, a flow and return fuel system was added with the introduction of the Quadrajet in 1968. A large aluminum-cased AC GF432 filter was mounted on a bracket in front of the air filter. The larger top outlet was connected to the carburetor, while the second outlet routed excess fuel back to the tank via a return line.

The Rochester carburetor carries its part number stamped vertically on the driver's side of the body towards the rear. On the base 300hp unit this was 7028207 on the manual car and 7028208 on the automatic. Rochester Quadrajet carburetors are also dated. They use the Julian calendar system in which the day of the year, 1-365, is followed by the last digit of the year. Thus 033-8 would be February 2 1968. Up to the end of 1975 the fourth character of the Rochester carburetor number denotes its year. Late in 1968 Carter started manufacturing the Quadrajet to assist Rochester meet the demand; these carburetors have Carter Quadrajet on the body.

As if to boost sales prospects for the aftermarket vendors of aluminum replacements, a single and unlovely iron intake manifold, cast with the number 3919803, was the only small-block manifold for 1968. As mentioned above, it had for the last time on a Corvette the hole to receive the oil filler tube cast in at the front, beside the coolant outlet neck.

Cylinder heads on the base 300hp 327 were part number 3917291. This was the first small-block head to carry a coolant temperature sensor. Previously the sensor had been located at the front of the intake manifold. There it had often failed to warn of high temperature if the coolant level was also low; not uncommon on earlier Corvettes. The new location, between exhaust ports for cylinders 3 and 5, allowed the sensor to remain immersed in the coolant even when well depleted. Valve covers were painted Chevrolet orange and lacked the traditional Chevrolet script now that they were perforated for the PCV (Positive Crankcase Ventilation) system.

As usual with the 300hp since its 1962 introduction as the first stage optional engine, intake valve heads were a generous 1.94in, with 1.5in exhaust valves. Flat-topped impact extruded or forged alloy pistons combined with 63.30cc combustion chambers yielded a 10.0:1 compression ratio. The camshaft was identified by a horizontal diamond symbol and was cast with the number 3896930, or more likely the last four digits of it – 6930. Lift on this hydraulic cam was .390in, with duration of 346° for intake valve opening and 320° for exhaust valve opening.

300 horsepower? Climb out of your 1993 300hp LT1 Corvette and into a 1968 base engined car and you will notice, among other things, a power deficiency in the older car. This is due to the changes in declared power measurement that took place in 1972 (to be discussed in Chapter 4). It is sufficient to say at this point that until 1971 power was measured with a perfect, blueprinted, ported and polished engine with no power-robbing ancillaries such as alternator, air injection pump and water pump, and probably with an optimistic eye on the dynamometer dial too. Since 1972, motors have been measured as installed, with all the belt-driven ancillaries.

Only one 327 cylinder block was used in 1968. Cast on the driver's side upper rear face with the number 3914678, this block had the familiar 4.00in bore and was also used, with a longer stroke, as a

350 in 1968 Camaros and Chevy IIs. Unlike previous 327s, it had no crankcase breather hole beside the distributor, all 1968 engines now having valve cover mounted PCV systems.

One of the few one-year-only motor parts in Corvette history, the 1968 crankshaft is unique and therefore hard to find. Known as the large journal 327 crank, its five main bearing journals were 2.45in and the rod journals 2.10in, the same as the 1969 and later 350 crankshafts. The stroke remained the standard 3.25in. This crankshaft was forged steel, like all Corvette 327 cranks before it.

Exhaust manifolds for 1968 small-blocks were number 3872765 left-hand and 3872778 right-hand. This was the last year in which the alternator was mounted via a cast boss on the front of the left-hand exhaust manifold; from 1969 the front of the head would be have three tapped holes for this purpose. All 1968s were equipped with Air Injection Reactor systems to reduce emissions (although most have since been removed) so the exhaust manifolds were tapped to receive the AIR fittings.

Base engine this may have been, but to today's owner who wants to use his car the 300hp has great appeal. It was very torquey, delivering 360lb ft at only 3600rpm, so it would easily pull a tall 3.08 rear axle ratio for fast and peaceful drives, while the fairly gentle cam can deliver around 20 miles per US gallon on a run.

L79 327 350hp The only optional small-block engine since 1966, the 327/350 introduced in 1965 is still a legend. Hungry for revs, it would scream its way to the redline in any gear with its perfect combination of big valves, aggressive cam and 11.0:1 compression. Demanding the best high-octane gasoline, it will detonate embarrassingly on today's unleaded unless the octane is boosted with the best additives. This was the kind of engine which Zora Arkus-Duntov liked best, a road circuit engine with instant response.

A little of the L79's visual sparkle was lost in the 1968 changeover. Gone were the beautifully sculpted high-rise aluminum intake manifold and the cast ribbed aluminum valve covers, though both would return in 1969. The carburetor was the Rochester Quadrajet, numbered 7028219 only, because no automatic was offered with this engine.

Almost unique among small-block Corvettes, the 1968 327 350 had chrome-plated valve covers.

The gold-finished vacuum cylinder at the left operated the windshield wiper flap.

The intake manifold was the cast iron unit used on the 300hp.

Sweat-shops in the Far East have been stamping out thin and leaky chrome-plated valve covers for small-block Chevy engines for years and it is easy to assume that the Corvette never used such an item. Virtually all small-block Corvette valve covers were stamped steel, painted engine color, or were cast aluminum. But here is the one exception: for the 1968 327/350, Chevrolet took the base engine's stamped covers and had them flash chromed.

The 3917292 head came with 2.02in diameter intake and 1.60in exhaust valves, and 63.99cc combustion chambers. Combined with forged pistons with a domed section and reliefs for high speed valve clearance, the result was a compression ratio of 11:1.

The camshaft was the traditional part number 3863151, cast 3863152 with a vertical diamond casting symbol. This is usually considered to be the hydraulic version of the legendary Duntov solid lifter cam. Lift on this hydraulic cam was .447in, with duration of 342° for both intake and exhaust valve openings. The 2in-outlet exhaust manifolds

were shared with the base 300hp motor.

Compared to the previous year's version, this L79 was breathing through a basic cast iron intake manifold and using just 2in exhaust manifolds. Even allowing for this author's preference for the Quadrajet over the Holley 4150, it is still hard to see how Chevrolet could rate this motor as a 350hp, but then they were probably thinking that anyone looking for real performance would be buying one of the five optional big-block engines anyway. If the N11 off-road exhaust system was specified, then this came with special mufflers and 2.5in pipes.

Today, many 327/350s have been tamed to run on pump gasoline, with lower-compression pistons, ignition timing backed off and gentler cams. That way they are definitely more driveable, but to wind up a correctly assembled L79 327/350, running full ignition advance and 100 octane gas, is one of the great Corvette experiences.

L36 427 390hp The big-block era lasted for just ten years of the Corvette's long and still continuing history, from 1965 to 1974. A total of about 71,000 big-block Corvettes were built in this period. Though peak sales were attained in the extended 1969 model year, the engine was at its most popular in 1968 when it accounted for no less than 44 per cent of Corvette production.

To understand why a well balanced car, with 45/55 front/rear weight distribution for 1967, and a well developed chassis, should need a big-block engine fitted, one must look at the car culture of the time. The dominant motor sport at the time was drag racing, from factory backed entries at national level to small town evening meets where all the racers were in their daily-driver cars. Drag racing is the most accessible of motor sports; it needs less marshals, less land, less equipment and less organization than almost any other, and for the competitor it offers very little risk except to the driveline.

The Corvette was never designed for drag racing. The rear wheel spindles were fine for road use, but too small in diameter to take the loads imposed by a full throttle launch and subsequent full-power shifts on sticky oversized tyres. Although the Corvette's independent rear suspension was always a winner on the bumpy blacktop at the down-town traffic light grand prix, it was better to substitute a complete Pontiac live rear axle to win on the quarter mile. Nevertheless, the Corvette was recruited into the muscle car horsepower race in competition with Chevrolet's own Camaro and Chevelle SS, which could both be ordered with the 396 big-block, with their Pontiac GTO and Firebird 400, Oldsmobile 4-4-2 and even the Buick GS 400.

General Motors has always been good at building the cars people want, not the ones they should want, so when they demanded horsepower GM made sure they got it with arguably the best of all the muscle car motors, the Mark IV Rat.

Properly referred to as the Mark IV big-block, this engine traced its ancestry back to the 348-409cu in W-block family of engines introduced in 1958. They were distinguished by their unusual 74° deck angle and the 348 was the performance option in the full size Chevrolet from that date. In 1961 a new 409 followed and from this was developed the 427cu in Z11, a W-block based race engine fitted into a 2-door Impala with dual four-barrel carburetors, cold air cowl induction and an incredible 13.5:1 compression ratio. This motor probably developed much more than its declared 430hp. The Z11 package was aimed squarely at the drag racing fraternity, and the Corvette never used the W-engine, thanks to Zora Arkus-Duntov's rightful preference for lighter, high revving engines.

In 1963 at Daytona a new Chevrolet race-only powerplant was unveiled, dubbed the Mark II, which combined the essentials of the Z11's bottom end with a 90° deck block and all-new cylinder

The tachometer redline varies according to the engine fitted. This redline (left) at 5600rpm was used only with hydraulic-lifter 390hp and 400hp big-blocks.

Less than 20% of 1968s were air conditioned, but the system was powerful and effective. The GF432 fuel filter was used only on 327 engines. The third pipe was the return to the tank.

heads. These used ball-mounted rockers like the small-block's, but the studs and valves were angled to allow a 'semi-hemi' type of combustion chamber, in order to accommodate bigger valves and improved inlet and exhaust ports.

GM management remembered the AMA ban on factory sponsored racing and the so-called 'mystery' motor was shelved. Behind the scenes, however, it was being developed, downsized to below the then Corporate maximum of 400cu in, and within two years was put into production at the Tonawanda, New York, plant, to replace the W-engine permanently.

In the L36 390hp big-block the block was cast number 3916321, replaced in January 1968 by the very similar 3935439. It had a bore of 4.25in and

1968 was the last year for an intake manifold-mounted oil filler. The air injection reactor (AIR) has been temporarily removed on this car, but they were factory fitted to all 1968 Corvettes.

Cylinder heads were cast number 3917215 and used 2.06in intake and 1.72in exhaust valves. These heads had the smaller 'oval' intake ports and were tapped to accept temperature sending units. Combined with domed cast alloy pistons with valve reliefs the compression ratio of the 1968 L36 was 10.25:1

The camshaft, cast number 3904359, gave intake and exhaust valve lift of .461in and .480in respectively, and duration of 350° and 352°, with a 1.7 rocker ratio. On big-blocks only the pushrods are different lengths because of the offset rocker studs, the lengths being 8½in intake and 9¾in exhaust. It is not uncommon for big-block rockers to break and sometimes bend a pushrod, so experienced big-block drivers pack a spare of each length, a rocker and two wrenches just in case.

The 19-tooth crankshaft sprocket had an extra tooth compared to the 327, so the cam sprocket had 38 teeth. The harmonic balancer was of 8in diameter, with no counterweight because unlike the later 454 the 427 engines are internally balanced.

Exhaust manifolds were designed to enhance gas flow, a complex casting keeping the flows separate until terminating in a 2½in 3-stud outlet. The left-hand manifold was cast number 3880827, the right 3880828, carried over from the previous two years. These manifolds were drilled and tapped for the AIR fittings used on all 1968s. Few take the risk with old manifolds today, but no gaskets were originally used against the cylinder head.

The distributor was just the same design as the small-block; it had single points and vacuum advance and was wrapped with a 1111293 label. The plug wires were shielded in all but the few cars where a radio was not fitted, and unlike on the 1965-67 big-block cars, the shielding braids were connected in pairs to the lower valve cover bolts.

L68 427 400hp The Tri-Power carburetor system had been introduced the previous year, to give better mixture distribution than was possible with the four-barrel. Universally called Tri-Power by Corvetteers, the nomenclature is more correctly the property of sister division Pontiac, who had been the first to use the system back in 1956.

The system consisted of three two-barrel Holley 2300Cs, normally used singly on low-output passenger car V8s, assembled onto a special cast aluminum manifold. Only the central carburetor was connected to the throttle cable, the front and rear units being controlled by vacuum diaphragms linked by hoses. The mechanical linkage between the carburetors was devised only to close, not to open, the front and rear units when the driver lifted his foot from the pedal. To ensure good idle and fresh fuel in the outer bowls, the idle system was constantly active in the secondary units. Each unit had its own internal fuel filter. On the manual-

two-bolt main bearing caps, which supported the forged steel crankshaft (cast number 7115). This had a stroke of 3.76in, making the engine well over-square. Connecting rods were 6.135in long, probably forged steel with 'double dimple' identification on the shank, magnafluxed and heat treated.

Intake air was filtered by a chrome-plated 14in round open-element cleaner with AC A212 CW element, and the carburetor was a Rochester Quadrajet numbered 7028209, or 7028216 if used with Turbo Hydra-Matic. The intake manifold was aluminum and carried the cast number 3919849, changing to 3937793 in the spring of 1968.

The big-block valve covers were chrome-plated from 1968 to 1970 only and were retained by seven bolts with special triangular washers. To help lubricate the ball pivot of the rockers, drippers were spot-welded to the inside of each cover, to catch oil mist and drop it directly onto each rocker. These welds tended to show as a dimple on the outside of the cover. Clips were spot-welded to the outside of each cover to mount the plug wire separators. The left cover was shaped to accommodate the optional brake booster of the previous year's car and carried over until about January of 1968 when the shaped depression, unnecessary with the new bodystyle, became less pronounced.

transmission car the center carburetor with the choke was Holley list number R4055, stamped 3925517 on early examples and 3940929 later. The front and rear units were R3659A, stamped 3902353. On cars equipped with the automatic transmission the center unit was changed to a Holley R4056A, stamped 3902516, and changed to the same 3940929 as the four-speed later.

With the idle jets well distributed across the manifold and the primaries centrally placed, the low-speed and part-throttle performance was good, while at wide-open throttle the combination could deliver 1000cfm to eight eager cylinders. The unit was topped off by a dramatic triangular chromed air filter with a washable sponge element. The manifold was cast number 3919850 in early production, and 3937795 later in 1968. Intake ports were oval on this 400hp unit to match the 3917215 heads.

Chevrolet reckoned the 3 x 2 Tri-Power carburetor set-up was worth 10hp, for the L68 was in most other respects identical to the L36 390hp described previously. However, the cylinder block, cast number 3916321 early and 3935439 late, was converted to 4-bolt main bearing caps. The distributor was the same 1111293 unit as on the 390hp. With peak torque of 460lb ft. at only 3600rpm this was a supremely powerful engine and one of the few on which the super-tall 2.73:1 axle ratio was offered, and then only with automatic transmission.

L71 427 435hp The next step up the optional performance ladder took the owner into the serious realms of the solid-lifter camshaft and ultra-high compression ratios, which, combined with the 1000cfm potential of the 3 x 2 Tri-power, added up to the most powerful engine ever offered in a Corvette. From the top, the motor looked just the same as the 400 horsepower, and was distinguished from it only by the 'Turbo-Jet - 3 x 2 - 435' label on the triangular air cleaner. Beneath it, even the carburetor numbers matched those on its hydraulic-liftered sibling.

The intake manifold, however, was different (cast number 3919852 early and 3937797 late), having larger, square ports to match the large-port high-performance cylinder head (cast number 3919840). These heads had massive 2.19in intake and 1.72in exhaust valves, as big as valves get in Chevrolets. With symmetrical-dome 435hp forged pistons the compression ratio was a starter-motor challenging 11.0:1.

Connecting rods were upgraded with a floating pin design, with retainers, for reduced friction at the piston. The solid lifter camshaft, cast number 3904366, gave a lift of .562in intake and .584in exhaust, with duration of 316° and 302° degrees respectively. The casting symbol was OMO. This engine developed its peak power at 5300rpm, with peak torque of 460lb ft at 4000rpm.

Redline on the tachometer was at a mind-boggling 6500rpm, about 2000rpm above what any wise driver would dare consider today. Back in 1968, when I was playing at being a hippy in California and driving a 1960 Ford Galaxy Sunliner Convertible, rated at a wildly optimistic 390hp from a meagre 352cu in (and we think GM exaggerated), I was well aware that guys with real money could buy my dream car – a '68 427 convertible with 435 Tri-Power and a four-speed - for under $4000. They could drag race every Friday night, wind it out to the redline and beyond, all under the GM warranty. The weak link in the big-block was always the connecting rods, and they regularly exited through the block due to over-revving. No wonder then that it is so hard today to find a genuinely 'matching numbers' 427, nor is it surprising that so many high-horsepower Corvettes have been happily but mysteriously reunited with their original engines, years after they were replaced under warranty!

L89 427 435hp The L89 435 was barely a full optional engine, just a head substitution on the L71, but the fitting of aluminum heads made for an enormously desirable car. The cylinder head in question was cast number 3919842. It was very similar in design to the cast iron 3919840 of the L71 but weighed a full 36lb less, leading to a 72lb weight saving on the car, and mainly at the front end where the saving was most needed. It was almost the same as the 1967 3904392 aluminum head too, but now had a tapped boss to accept the more sensibly located temperature sender.

Even better was the improved thermal efficiency of the head. Being more conductive, it prevented hot spots and therefore pre-ignition. This allowed the engine to accept more ignition advance, and therefore make more power. Since the disappearance from the pumps of high-test leaded gas these heads have shown their third great advantage - they are ideal for re-tuning a big-block to run on unleaded. But perhaps the best feature of all is the long-term one. Crack a cast iron head and it is finished, almost certainly beyond repair. Aluminum, however, is easy to weld, and since the late 1960s welding techniques and equipment have improved, too.

In 1968, Chevrolet assembled 2898 L71s, of which 624 were factory fitted with aluminum heads to make them L89s. So if you ordered an L71 new back in 1968, and then learned at your first service that your dealer could upgrade your car to an absolutely correct L89 simply by changing the heads, you might well have done it. After five years you would probably believe that your car always had been an L89. You would have sold it quite honestly as a L89 back in 1972 when family semed more important than sports cars, and the car would

IDENTIFICATION

Engine block cast numbers
327cu in   3914678
427cu in   3916321 for 390/400/430/435hp
                  3935439 for 430/435hp

Stamped engine number suffixes
HE   327-300hp   Rochester 4BC manual
HO   327-300hp   Rochester 4BC auto
HI   327-350hp   Rochester 4BC spec high perf, manual
HP   327-350hp   Rochester 4BC spec high perf, manual, AC, PAS.
IL   427-390hp   Rochester 4BC hydr. lifters, manual
IQ   427-390hp   Rochester 4BC hydr. lifters, auto
IM   427-400hp   Holley 3x2BC manual
IO   427-400hp   Holley 3x2BC auto
IR   427-435hp   Holley 3x2BC mech. lifters, manual
IU   427-435hp   L89.Holley 3x2BC, mech. lifters, manual, alloy heads
IT   427-430hp* L88.Holley 4BC, mech. lifters, M22 manual

*probably 560bhp

Chassis numbers
194378S400001 through 194378S428566 (4th digit for a convertible is 6)

change hands many times through the '80s as a genuine L89. Only when your car is bought by a high-roller collector who sees it as an investment, and sends his newly acquired rarity to a restorer, does the truth come out. The casting date on the heads is newer than the car's build date and the angry collector calls his attorney because he is mad as hell, he has been sold a fake and he needs to get even. Unfortunately, without written evidence from all the previous owners and an original invoice, it is almost impossible to be sure that an L89 is genuine, and it is a brave appraiser who puts his name behind one.

L88 427 '430hp' With the exception of the possibly unique and almost mythical 1969 ZL1, there was never a more powerful carbureted Corvette motor than the 1967-69 L88. This was a motor designed to offer the ultimate in big-block performance. It was built for use on the track and was based broadly on the L71. The carburetor was the racer's favorite, a monster Holley R4054A, stamped 3925519, on an aluminum intake manifold (cast number 3885069 or later 3933198).

Its aluminum cylinder heads were the L89's 3904392, and with the massively domed forged pistons used these gave a compression ratio of 12.5:1. Specified idle speed was 1000rpm and the fuel had to be a minimum 103 research octane. The camshaft was part number 3928909 and cast number 3928911. Intake valve lift was .562in, exhaust .584in, with duration of 354° and 360° respectively. Even the pushrods were oversized at $\frac{7}{16}$in.

Despite its obvious destiny as a race car the L88 was sold with road equipment and therefore the same PCV and AIR equipment as its stablemates. Induction was through a special cold air hood which took high-pressure air from the foot of the windshield and filtered it through a hood-mounted

filter. An air filter base was still mounted to the top of the carburetor, with a deep foam seal around its perimeter and small flame guard to protect the hood against blow back. Other options were required to complete the package including J56 special heavy-duty power brakes, F41 front and rear suspension, K66 transistor ignition, and radio deletion to discourage street driving. The radiator was aluminum, smaller than the usual copper/brass big-block unit, and was installed without a shroud but with an expansion tank. Only 80 L88s were built and Chevrolet avoided mentioning a horsepower figure. It was probably in excess of 550hp. Amazingly, the L88 was offered with automatic transmission.

COOLING SYSTEM

Aluminum radiators by Harrison Industries were used only on the base 300hp and L79 350hp 327 engines, and then only if fitted with manual transmissions and no air conditioning, and also on the L88 described above. Coolant filling on these was via the aluminum expansion tank, made by Harrison Industries and stamped 3016340, located behind the right-hand inner fender. The filler cap was an AC RC-26. Small-block cars with aluminum radiators had a pressed steel shroud, but the L88 had none.

All other 1968s used a conventional copper radiator with end tanks, no separate expansion tank, and an AC RC-15 cap. A fiberglass radiator shroud was used with all copper radiators. For various reasons the new-shape Corvettes were prone to overheating, particularly big-blocks. This was the first time that a Corvette was designed in which the majority of the radiator's cooling air was designed to be drawn from under the car rather than through the grille. Though the grille still existed, it had a very small area and was effectively blocked by the closed headlamps and their dirt shields. It is well documented by Karl Ludvigsen that even just before the model launch the cooling was insufficiently tested and that the two large holes were cut by hand in the lower front panel. The NCRS Judging Manual suggests that some cars, particularly big-blocks, were recalled to make this modification. The spoiler behind was also said to have been added at the last minute as production was commencing. The AIR system, wider use of air conditioning and even increasing traffic congestion all contributed to the problem. Additional rubber seals around the shroud were also added to help the fan draw only through the radiator.

EMISSION SYSTEM

All 1968 Corvettes were built with an air injection reactor (AIR) system installed, even the race-only

L88. They also had positive crankcase ventilation (PCV), something all Corvettes had had since the first Sting Rays. The AIR pump was belt driven and forced fresh air into the exhaust manifolds to promote a secondary burn of the combustion gases in the exhaust system and thus reduce emission of unburned hydrocarbons. To prevent backfire under certain conditions, such as engine overrun, a vacuum-controlled diverter valve dumped the pressurised air via a small silencer. Undoubtedly the ugliest engine accessory ever devised, the pump and its associated plumbing and valves were discarded wholesale by enthusiastic owners, this one included. For originality, the whole system should be in place.

ELECTRICS

The new shape 1968 Corvette had more lamps, more bulbs, more relays and more wire to connect them all up than ever before. The quality of the wiring harness was excellent, the fusebox less so and subject to long-term corrosion. Electrical power was generated by a 12-volt alternator with external voltage controller. The unit was pivoted on a bracket fixed to the left-hand exhaust manifold. Adjustment of belt tension was by a bracket which extended to the water pump.

The Delcotron 10 DN alternator had been introduced in 1963 and made its last appearance for 1968. It was a beautifully made and wonderfully reliable unit that would serve until replaced by a new design with a solid-state internal voltage controller in 1969.

Because alternators are invariably needed in a hurry, they tend to be replaced by rebuilt exchange units with the wrong numbers and often of the wrong type. On cars without air conditioning or transistor ignition a 37amp 5.5in aluminum Delcotron, stamped 1100693/37, was used. Transistor ignition cars used a 42amp unit stamped 1100696/42. Air-conditioned cars used a 61amp unit stamped 1100750/61. As with so many parts on a Corvette these were also stamped with a date of manufacture, then to assist quality control and now important to us in the search for authenticity and accurate restoration. Date stamping was year/month/day on the front case.

The ignition distributor used on 1968 Corvettes was a Delco Remy, with the number on a tag wrapped around the base. It had a cast iron base and a vacuum advance canister with rubber and steel piping to the carburetor. There was a horizontal gear drive and fittings for the cable which drove the tachometer, unique to the Corvette and Camaro with optional tachometer. All distributors used a black cap with an inspection window through which dwell adjustments could be made with the engine running by using an Allen wrench. This operation adjusted the contact breaker points.

Twin tail lights had been a Corvette icon most years since 1961; now they made they last appearance until 1984.

On any engine except the base 300 hp it was possible to order K66 transistor ignition. Usually referred to as TI, it had been a popular option since its 1964 introduction. This magnetic-based system used a special Delcotronic distributor, still with mechanical tachometer drive, and a transistor amplifier mounted on the radiator support bracket. It had the advantage of providing a stronger and better timed spark throughout the range from cold start to peak revs, and did not require the frequent replacement of the contact breaker points, but it was a mystery to most service stations and was dropped after 1969.

On small-blocks the ignition wires were routed down behind the engine and up underneath the ram's horn style cast iron exhaust manifolds. The spark plug boots were protected from heat radiated by the manifolds by J-shaped heat shields. On the majority of cars which were fitted with radios the wires were covered by shielding. Big-block cars used a shield on the distributor only, because the wires were encased in a stainless steel braid, which was grounded to the top shield and to the lower valve cover bolts.

The Corvette radio was unique in the Chevrolet range, an AM/FM unit offered in a choice of mono or stereo, with adjustable pre-set tuning buttons and volume and tuning knobs which matched the rest of the dash. The transistor pack was separate from the receiver and mounted on a heat sink on the firewall. The antenna was a subtly tapered fixed length mast, boosted by an aluminum ground plane, with no power option. Retained by a nut, it was easily removed for parking.

For 1968 two previously alien systems were introduced: fiber optics for external lamp

Twin back-up lamps were mounted below the bumper for 1968 only.

monitoring and vacuum for control of heating, ventilation, air conditioning and external moving surfaces. If that sounds like something from the airplane industry, then the stylists succeeded in their aims. Undoubtedly they would have liked to provide a vacuum controlled rear spoiler and vacuum operated flip-up brake lights too, but we must be forever grateful that we got the moving surfaces we did. The flip-up headlamps work reliably and well, powered by big reversible vacuum actuators, which in turn were controlled by vacuum relays. This system proved itself by being used with virtually no changes until the model end in 1982. Over-rides and a reservoir were incorporated, the latter allowing for operation after the vacuum source, the engine, was switched off.

The otherwise conventional windshield wipers and washer system were cleverly hidden by a lifting flap. Pushing the console mounted switch was all that was required to signal the vacuum actuator to raise the flap. This in turn pressed a relay which signalled the wipers to start. Switching off the engine triggered a shutdown sequence which is still impressive. More complex than the headlamps, this system was less reliable but always remained operable by using the over-rides under the steering column. An auto-electrician and friend, now sadly departed, once pointed out to me that vacuum work on a Corvette is easy if you leave it to an electrician. The hoses are color coded, well mapped in the shop manual, and they are 'either live or not'. To make any vacuum job easier, leave the engine turned off and use an external source, even another car at idle with a long hose.

The lamp monitor system checked all the external lighting except back-up and side markers. Fiber optic cable was led to small lenses in the reflector of each lamp, then to the front and rear lamp displays at the front and rear of the shift console. Effective and simple, we thought that one day all cars would have this, but they didn't and fiber optic cable became instead a revolutionary communications medium. Latterly the monitor system has been a useful pointer to old crash damage - a dead monitor and a live lamp indicate where the damage was repaired but the monitor optic cable usually was not!

On 1968s only the front marker lamps have a clear plastic lens with an amber bulb. At the rear, four round red tail lamps had been a Corvette trademark since 1961. Since 1991 we have had four squircle shaped lenses, and then since '97 four ovals, but they all mean Corvette when spotted on the freeway at night. Two of the lamps were lost to back-up lamps in 1966, but a separate central white lens restored them for 1967. Now the back-up lights were paired under the rear bumper.

Ask a Corvette dealer what he thinks is the worst feature on a 1968-82 and he will tell you without hesitation - the battery location behind the driver's seat. To see why, just try hooking jump leads onto the battery of a four-speed car that has stood for a few weeks, and then climb in to press the clutch pedal and start it! When we were shown the new 1984 C4 at a private European dealer preview in Switzerland in 1983, I was at the front of the line to see it and Dave McLellan personally showed me the car. He wanted me to see the new and much improved interior, but I am ashamed to say that my first words were 'Forget the interior, where's the battery?' Fortunately, it is under the hood on both the C4 and the new C5!

TRANSMISSIONS

Presumably to help the dealer to offer a competitive start price, and definitely to help GM make extra profit, the base Corvette was delivered with a less than desirable three-speed manual transmission, the essential four-speed starting at an extra $184.35.

The three-speed was sold in just over 300 of the 28,556 1968s. Many will have been converted to four-speed, so they are now rare. This cast iron transmission was a built at Saginaw, Michigan, and had been revised in 1966 to incorporate synchromesh on all forward gears. Ratios were wide, with a 2.54:1 first gear. The main case casting number was 3925647 and the extension 3860042. The shifter had no reverse lock-out handle as seen on the four-speeds.

The aluminum-cased Muncie four-speed had been the most popular Corvette transmission since it replaced the Warner T-10 in 1963. It is one of those legendary American products, tough and simple but beautiful to look at, often abused but supremely reliable. It is readily identified from early or late T-10s by its seven retaining bolts on the side cover, and the characteristic brick-like projection on the top back of the main case. It had three shift levers, forward speeds on the side cover and reverse on the extension housing.

The Muncie was available three ways in 1968 as an M20 wide-ratio with 2.52:1 first gear, an M21 close-ratio with 2.20:1 first, or the heavy-duty Rock Crusher M22, fitted only to the L88. Identification was only by annular rings machined on the input shaft, provided this has not been replaced in a previous repair. The M20 had two rings, M21 one ring and M22 none. All inputs had a 10-groove spline.

The 1968 main case was cast number 3925660, the side cover 3884685 and the extension housing 3857584. The main case was stamped vertically on the rear right of the main case with a plant code and assembly date, and on a second line the Corvette's partial VIN number starting at the sixth, year, character.

The shifter was all chrome with a lifting T-handle to lock out reverse gear and a heavy chrome knob. The earlier shift vibration problem had been solved in 1967 by mounting the unit via a bracket direct to the chassis, but there is often an interference problem between the shifter and the console.

The flywheel and diaphragm clutch were of 10.4in diameter for the small-block cars and 11.0in for big-blocks, both with a coarse spline driven plate. The mechanical clutch mechanism was easy and simple to maintain. The upper clutch pushrod operated the cross shaft, which was mounted on ball studs - one screwed into the cylinder block, the other on a frame mounted tower. This tower was not fitted to frames on automatic cars. The cross shaft was linked to the clutch fork by a lower link with anti-rattle springs.

Adjusted by a pair of easily accessible jam nuts on the upper pushrod, and proven in millions of other Chevrolets, the clutch is one more of those tough but simple components which make the Corvette such a pleasure to own. When replacement is required, only the bell housing and transmission need to be removed to change it.

The 1968 Corvette was the first to be fitted with a three-speed automatic transmission. The two-speed Powerglide was replaced by the three-speed Turbo Hydra-Matic 400, first used in other Chevrolets in 1965. Optioned with the RPO code M40, this was a serious heavy-duty unit, generally regarded as one of the best and used in a wide range of vehicles from trucks to Rolls-Royces and Jaguars. Gear selection was by cable from a chrome shifter rod with a black plastic knob, and kickdown

was also by cable. This transmission is capable of hundreds of thousands of miles of service with only routine fluid and filter changes.

The differential was mounted centrally and solidly to its own rubber-isolated cross-member. The front yoke and therefore the propshaft were offset by one inch from the centerline of the car. At the front, the engine was offset by the same amount to allow more foot and pedal room for the driver.

The base differential was a 3.36:1 ratio, supplied with the three-speed 'box or the M20 wide-ratio

The futuristic option PO1 Bright Metal Wheel Covers were dramatic and popular, but the future of wheel styling turned out to be deep dish instead. All 1968 wheels were 7 x 15 steel.

'box, and 3.70:1 with the M21 close-ratio. If automatic was ordered then this came with a 3.08:1 unit. Positraction limited slip was optional in a wide range of ratios: 3.08:1, 3.36:1, 3.55:1, 3.70:1 and 4.11:1. The rare 2.73:1 was only available in Positraction and only with automatic and 427 big-block. With this ratio the motor would be turning at a relaxed 2500rpm at 75mph. The Positraction friction plates require a special GM lubricant and additive for smooth operation as well as to avoid low-speed chatter and clonks when hot.

WHEELS & TIRES

A new-look slotted wheel had been launched for the 1967 Sting Ray. Called the Rally wheel, it broke with the full wheel-cover tradition (where the wheel had been hidden by a full cover). With rim width increased to 7in for 1968 and manufactured by Kelsey Hayes, the 15in Rally wheel had five oval slots and was painted a slightly greenish shade of silver, the inside face being black.

The outer trim ring was polished stainless steel and retained by four clips. Because Chevrolet balance weights were only fitted to the inside rim of the wheel, there was no interference problem with the clips. The center cap was a combination of chromed diecast and stainless steel and bore the legend Chevrolet Motor Division. It clipped onto pressed lugs on the wheel and was removable with strong fingers.

An optional P01 Bright Metal Wheel Cover cost an extra $57.95 a set. It was quite different to anything previously offered, a futuristic vision with 72 fins radiating from a cross-flagged center emblem. Valve extensions with no valve caps were needed to fill the tire with air, and were supplied in the glovebox with the new car. They marked a wheel design direction which no one else would follow, but were ordered by more than 30 per cent of 1968 buyers. In later years they were almost never seen on the road, only piled high and offered cheap at swapmeets, but their fortunes have been revived by the interest in restoration and originality, and by the number of owners who have found their tank stickers showing the P01 as fitted originally to their cars.

Wider wheels meant wider tires, and the base tire for 1968 was a blackwall F70x15 bias-ply nylon cord by Firestone, Goodyear or Uniroyal. Driving a car on bias-belt nylon tires today is an interesting experience because the ride, steering feel and wet traction are so incredibly bad. Leaving aside originality, Corvettes are high-performance cars and need modern radial tyres. Whitewall tires would no longer be fitted to Corvettes, for the age of the stripe tire had dawned. Optional tires were narrow white stripes or narrow red stripe Firestone Wide O Oval, Goodyear Wide Tread F70-15 or UniRoyal Tiger Paw.

SUSPENSION & STEERING

The all-new body of the 1968 was fitted to an all old chassis. Indeed, with just a few days work it is theoretically possible to interchange the bodies of a 1967 and a 1968. The chassis was actually introduced in September 1962 and the front suspension was based on existing production components from other model lines of the time. In fact the upper control arms and front hubs were from the 1958-64 full-size car.

The front suspension used rubber-bushed unequal-length upper and lower control or A-arms linked by balljoints to a forged one-piece knuckle and spindle, which was also shared with the full-size car. Castor and camber were easily adjusted by shims inserted between the upper control arm pivot and its mounting on the frame. Springs were conventional coils, working between the lower control arms and shallow towers in the frame. There were five different spring specifications according to the engine size and optional equipment, each marked with a green paper tag carrying the GM part number and two-letter broadcast code.

Shock absorbers were by Delco and were located inside the springs. They were painted blue-gray, carried the stamping Delco Remy, and were described in the original sales brochure as double-acting. Replacements, even from Delco, would normally have been single-acting, and would have been required quite early in the cars' life. When replacing shocks it is rare to find double-acting units fitted. A Corvette needs effective shocks and it is a shame that so few owners will have experienced the suspension the way it should have been.

A stabilizer, or sway, bar was fitted ahead of the front wheels, linking the lower control arms to bushes on the frame. Base suspension cars had a ½in diameter bar, while on 427s, or on the optional F-41, there was ¹⁵⁄₁₆in bar. Like the frame, this front suspension was well designed from the outset and would be fitted to two-thirds of a million cars by 1982. F41 cars used stiffer, shorter front coils and larger diameter shocks.

Base equipment for the Sting Ray was unassisted steering. It was conventional for the time, with a recirculating-ball steering box, track arm with four identical but handed rod ends, and an idler arm. The steering ratio could be varied because a choice of track rod end holes was provided in the steering arms. The rearmost position was used for the low-geared position, giving a standard ratio of 19.6:1, while the forward position gave the faster 17.0:1 ratio, also used when the car was fitted with option N40 power-assisted steering.

When the system was designed for the 1963 Corvette, integrated powered steering boxes were available, but the engineers wisely chose steering feel instead by opting for an outdated system first seen on the classic 1955 Chevrolet passenger car, and that was about to be superseded. It had a leak-prone control valve, which formed the link between the track arm and a separate ram with four external hydraulic hoses, but it gave assistance when required, was never intrusive at higher speeds and still allowed the front wheels to communicate road feel to the driver. It looked old fashioned in 1963 but was still being fitted to new Corvettes 19 years later.

In 1963 the new Corvette's fully independent rear suspension had been a sensation, and five years later it was still unique for a domestic car. American engines and transmissions had been superb for years, but the sports car enthusiast had been denied a vehicle which could really put that power to the ground. Show-off kids liked to light up one rear tire, drag racers fitted low-pressure slicks to accelerate in a straight line - and lost control if they started to turn - but here at last was a vehicle in which you could apply full power even on irregular surfaces and the wheels would just lock to the road and thrust the car forward.

The new 1963 rear suspension was beautifully simple - it had to be, otherwise Chevrolet would have refused to sanction its production on cost grounds alone. It was designed as a three-link system, following principles proven on Zora Arkus-Duntov's wonderful mid-engined CERV-1 experimental hill-climb special and sometime show car. In this car, the driveshaft between the differential and rear wheel spindle served as the top link of the lateral rear suspension parallelogram. This avoided the potentially troublesome splined sleeves that were required when the driveshafts had to vary in length as the suspension moved up and down.

Jaguar too used this principle in their XKE, but they engineered it with incredible complexity and presumably great expense. In the Corvette everything was as simple as possible. A fabricated trailing arm pivoted on a rubber bushing which was bolted into the frame just ahead of the rear wheel. This arm held the taper roller bearing spindle and hub assembly, and the brake, and handled the torque reactions from both. Shims at either side of the arm adjusted rear wheel toe-in.

The driveshafts had stout universal joints at either end and doubled as the upper lateral links. Right first time, and a parts man's dream, these universals were still in use on the 1996 Corvette, 23 years later. The bottom link, which completed the parallelogram, was a simple rubber-bushed steel bar joining a projection of the cast iron hub carrier to an eccentric adjuster on a bracket below the differential. To isolate the passenger compartment from any noise, the differential was rubber mounted by oversize cushions in its massive rear crossmember and by pairs of cushions either side of its front bracket.

Where the Jaguar rear suspension employed paired coil-over shocks on either side, the spring on the Corvette was a single nine-leaf transverse unit reminiscent of the Model-T Ford's. Bolted to the underside of the differential rear cover, it kept the center of gravity low, but required the dual exhaust pipes to unite beneath it to avoid conflict. A single high-tensile bolt with flat washers and rubber doughnut insulators connected each end of the under-hung spring to the trailing arms. These bolts offered easy ride height adjustment, using spacer washers to raise the rear of the car or longer bolts to lower it. The optional F41 suspension substituted a stiffer seven-leaf spring for the nine-leaf and incorporated a $\frac{9}{16}$in rear sway bar, also used on all big-blocks.

The right-angled extension of the lower hub carrier pivot shaft anchored the lower end of the shock absorber. The top was bolted through a bracket on the frame and fastened with a special thin nut to clear the adjacent body panel. The shock absorbers were double-acting, painted blue-gray and stamped the same as the front

The rear wheel spindle was a press fit into its two taper-roller bearings, which were pre-adjusted by a shim and spacer between their inner races. The press fit was a safety feature intended, in the days of drum brakes, to retain the wheel and spindle if the driveshaft assembly broke or otherwise parted from the spindle, and was not changed when disc brakes made it unnecessary. The Shop Manual required the rear wheel bearings to be repacked with grease every 30,000 miles, but because removing and replacing each rear driveshaft was a necessary part of this job, it was rarely done and rear wheel bearing failure was not uncommon.

Alignment of the rear end was achieved by spacers on either side of the trailing arm front pivot bolt. The difficulty of removing this bolt, which would rust itself permanently into the arm bushing retainer sleeve, would blight the Corvette for the next 20 years. Accidental impact of the wheels and general wear tended to make the rear wheels toe out over time, leading to that familiar feeling of instability that blights so many 1963-82s. On any car with independent rear suspension, rear alignment is as important as front, but once they are rusted in, removing those bolts to align the rear could become an eight-hour job and was seldom tackled. It was a shame that this aspect of the rear suspension was never improved.

BRAKES

The Corvette came of age as a performance car with the change to four-wheel disc brakes for the 1965 model year. To drivers bred on drum brakes, they were a revelation. Not just incredibly

OPTIONS

Code	Option	Quantity	Price
19437	Base Corvette Sport Coupe	9936	$4663.00
19467	Base Corvette Convertible	18630	$4320.00
L30	Base 327 300hp motor	5875	$0.00
base	Base three-speed	326	$0.00
base	Vinyl trim	26137	$0.00
-	Leather seats	2429	$79.00
A01	Soft Ray tinted glass, all windows	17635	$15.80
A02	Soft Ray tinted windshield	5509	$10.55
A31	Power windows	7065	$57.95
A82	Headrests	3197	$42.15
A85	Shoulder harness, std with coupe	350	$26.35
C07	Auxiliary Hardtop - 19467 only	8735	$231.75
C08	Auxiliary top exterior vinyl trim	3050	$52.70
C50	Rear window defroster	693	$31.60
C60	Air conditioning	5664	$412.90
F41	Special front & rear suspension	1758	$36.90
G81	Positraction rear axle, all ratios	27008	$42.15
J50	Power brakes	9559	$42.15
J56	Heavy duty brakes	81	$384.45
K66	Transistor ignition	5457	$73.75
L36	427 390hp engine	7717	$200.15
L68	427 400hp engine	1932	$305.50
L71	427 435hp engine	2898	$437.10
L79	327 350hp engine	9440	$105.35
L88	427 430hp engine	80	$947.90
L89	L71 with aluminum heads 435hp	624	$805.75
M20	Four-speed manual wide ratio	10760	$184.35
M21	Four-speed manual close ratio	12337	$184.35
M22	Four-speed manual heavy duty	80	$263.30
M40	Turbo Hydra-Matic transmission	5063	$226.45
N11	Off-road exhaust	4695	$36.90
N36	Telescopic steering column	6477	$42.15
N40	Power-assisted steering	12364	$94.80
P01	Full wheelcover	8971	$57.95
PT6	Red stripe tires F70 x15	11686	$31.30
PT7	White stripe tires F70 x 15	9692	$31.30
UA6	Alarm system	388	$26.35
U15	Speed warning Indicator	3453	$10.55
U69	AM/FM radio	24609	$172.75
U79	Stereo AM/FM radio	3311	$278.10

powerful, and capable of repeated stops from high speed, they were beautifully progressive too. They were designed to the very best standards of the time and without any compromise on performance.

The calipers were cast iron. To spread the load on the large friction pads equally, the caliper had four pistons, two each side, and was rigidly mounted. By contrast calipers on today's cars usually have pistons on one side only and an often troublesome sliding mount to compensate. The front pistons were of 1⅞in diameter and the rear 1⅜in, made of anodized aluminum. This established brake balance at 65/35 front to rear. Internal drillings ensured that there was only one external pressure feed, although the rear calipers each had two bleed screws. The rotors or discs were fully ventilated, 1¼in thick and of 11⅛in diameter. Annoyingly, front and rear had slightly different offsets, so they could not be interchanged.

A 1in bore Delco Moraine dual master cylinder was used. It was filled through a single lid retained with two wire clips. When J50 power assisted brakes were specified, the vacuum booster was painted black and took its vacuum from a fitting on the intake manifold.

The calipers were not designed with a parking brake in mind, so a small separate cable-operated drum-type brake was built into the centre offset of the rear rotor. Adjustment was made by a star wheel accessed through an inspection hole in the rotor and spindle flange. When rotors were changed during service, these holes were often not lined up, and then the parking brake could not be adjusted.

Long term, and mainly through lack of maintenance, the calipers and parking brake were both terribly troublesome. If the fluid in the brake system was changed regularly, preferably annually, then the calipers would last indefinitely. But brake fluid is hygroscopic, that is it absorbs water vapor from the atmosphere, and this water would condense in the calipers and start to rust the polished cast iron bores. Once the bores were pitted, no amount of re-sealing, cleaning or polishing would restore the seal.

A curious feature of the Corvette caliper is that they can be absolutely dry externally but cannot be bled successfully, and then even if a hard pedal is achieved it will collapse to the floor in a few miles. This happens because while the seal is sufficiently good to retain the fluid, external air is still drawn past the seal whenever the brake pedal makes its return or upward stroke. When this occurs, the fluid level in the reservoir will rise.

Happily, stainless steel sleeved exchange calipers were invented in about 1976, and have become cheaper every year since. Usually sold with a lifetime warranty, they are almost an essential on a good Corvette today. It is now cheaper for a shop to fit exchange stainless units than to attempt to re-seal the originals.

Hidden away inside the rotor, well away from regular maintenance, the parking or emergency brake also deteriorated fast. The operating levers rusted together and relied on a slot in the thin dust shield for location, but stainless steel mechanisms have effectively solved this problem. But if the 6.5in diameter drums of the emergency brake were relied on to stop the car, then a real emergency would surely follow, as the emergency brake is wholly unable to stop the car on the move.

J56 heavy-duty brakes were a mandatory option with the L88 and therefore the ZL1 too. The caliper was smooth topped with drillings for two pad locating pins. The twin pins provided better location for the pads, which were also reinforced with a folded top edge. The pistons in the J56 calipers only were the old 1965-66 long style with internal extensions which located into lugs in the caliper body. This helped the pistons to stay upright in extreme use.

1969

A 1968 owner contemplating a new Corvette for the spring of 1969 would certainly have been tempted in the showroom by a much improved car. It was clear that Chevrolet had been hard at work developing and refining their unique fiberglass sports car, because from any angle its stance was improved. It looked wider, more confident and even more aggressive than the previous year's model. This improved appearance was due to the new wider 8in Rally wheels. In three successive production years the wheel size had increased annually by an inch, and now the wheels really filled the arches. Tire size remained unchanged with the same F70 15 belted tires as the 1968, but stretching them onto the wider rim emphasised the fatness of the 70 profile, then the lowest profile that could be bought. These really showed off the white or red stripe tires factory fitted for the majority of buyers.

The front fenders were now adorned by new chrome-plated italic Stingray emblems. Now Corvettes could once again be called by an alternate name, and owners of 1968 models could quickly update their cars too. At the rear, the 1969 model lost its back-up lights, these now being incorporated with red reflectors into the space previously occupied by the inner pair of rear lamps. So now it was harder to spot those Corvettes at night again,

The 1969 Corvette was just as exciting as the 1968, and it was improved in dozens of ways, too.

Wider 8 x 15 wheels improved the stance of the car (above) while using the same F70 15 bias-ply tires as the previous 7 x 15 wheels. Only L88 427-powered big-blocks and the one, or maybe two, ZL1s got this special hood. Red stripe tires were last available in 1969 - ideal for a black car (right) with a red interior.

DIMENSIONS & WEIGHTS

Length	182.5in
Width	69.2in
Height	
Sport Coupe	47.75in
Convertible	47.8in
Wheelbase	98.0in
Max track	
Front	58.7in
Rear	59.4in
Curb weight	
Sport Coupe	3245lb
Convertible	3250lb

which probably saved a few tickets from being issued too.

Behind the front wheels, chromed die-cast trims could be now be ordered to emphasize the four vents. These were immediately popular and were easily and often retro-fitted to early '69s and of course '68s. They were only available from mid-December 1968, but had been shown as an option in the September sales brochure. Shown too in that brochure was the new N14 side exhaust, which would first be fitted from January 10 1969. First seen as a 1965 option and much missed in 1968, this loud side exhaust was something that no other mass-produced car offered as a factory option.

The showroom visitor would find the most impressive changes inside the car. Opening the door, he would notice the outside handles were simplified and easier to use, because the protruding push-knob needed to open the 1968 door was now gone, replaced by a mechanism neatly incorporated into the upper door handle flap. Once seated, the most significant change was the smaller black rimmed 15in diameter steering wheel, replacing the even then old fashioned 16in simulated woodgrain wheel of the 1968. An new optional tilt and telescopic steering column incorporating the ignition

switch, along with restyled door panels, made the 1969 interior much more appealing for the driver. The passenger would be less impressed by the token attempt at a map pocket on the fascia. It would be another nine years before a real glovebox was provided.

1969 was the most spectacular year for Corvette options with a total of 40 offered, if the convertible body is consideredan option and color choices are ignored. This does not mean that the cars would be any less well equipped, just that many of the options such as the four-speed gearbox would become standard.

The convertible body effectively became an option in 1969. In the years following the launch of the split-window coupe as an alternative body in 1963, the convertible had always outsold the closed car. In 1963 convertible sales had exceeded that sensational coupe by barely 300, but in 1967 and 1968 the convertible was outselling the coupe by two to one. Then in 1969 the situation quickly went into reverse and sales of the convertible rapidly lost ground to the coupe. This trend would continue, until the convertible represented less than a third of sales in 1971, less than a sixth in 1973, and less than an eighth by

Cars with the 427 big-block had a gently aggressive raised panel in the hood to provide clearance for the larger motor.

Only 116 L88s were built and all had this tall hood which ducted cold air from the base of the windshield to the carburetor. The air filter was built into the hood panel, which was protected from blow-back by the flame arrestor visible on the big Holley.

the end of 1975 production, after which it was not surprisingly discontinued.

The easy explanation is that the new for 1968 lift-out roof panels and easily removed back window offered the feeling of open-air driving with improved convenience and weatherproofing, but it is more likely that the sales reflected the enormous social and cultural changes happening in the United States at that time. Today a buyer looking for a convertible will not accept a coupe, even if the removable roof panels and rear window are demonstrated. The coupe will never feel like a true roadster.

A convertible demands short hair and suitable clothes, and open-air driving leads to a suntan and a red neck. Convertible drivers are outgoing, have to look cheerful, and can have no secrets. But from 1967 to 1969 a more introspective attitude began to prevail and the pale, long-haired and serious looking man or woman, now dressed in complicated and carefully considered clothing, became the fashion ideal. Such people travelled mysteriously, behind tinted glass and hiding their feelings behind sunglasses.

Music was now part of the affluent lifestyle and the car was turning into an entertainment center. A closed car was quieter at speed and a secure home

for the precious 8-track player and stereo tape cartridges, which were never safe beneath a folding roof. General Motors had predicted the trend and launched the 1970 F-body Camaro and Firebird with no open-roof option.

Corvette sales were improving too, though the exceptional 1969 total of 38,762 units sold was a reflection of a sales period which was extended by almost four months following a spring shutdown of the St Louis plant for a GM-wide labor strike which lasted from April 10 to June 9.

The 1969 Corvette is currently perceived by collectors, particularly of big-block cars, to be one of the high points of Corvette desirability. The cars are seen as the apogee of the pre-emission control era too, even though all '69s left the factory with the ugly AIR pumps installed. Certainly, changes from 1970 on would civilize the Corvette, and start to adapt it to a new generation of owners. It is no coincidence that at the time of writing 1969 also conforms to the Thirty Year Rule, precious to dealers. This theorem states that a classic car will reach its height of desirability 30 years after it is built, because the 15 year old who ached to own such a car 30 years before will now be 45, possibly with more independent children and as ready as he will ever be to afford the car.

BODY & BODY TRIM

The 1969 body itself was essentially unchanged from the previous year, but there were many minor trim changes. There were also the inevitable color and color name changes, with one race circuit, Silverstone, dropped but four new circuit names gained. 1969 would be last year for seven in which it was possible to order a Corvette in black.

Finish and panel fit was generally much improved over the previous year. Additional reinforcement flanges were introduced in front of

For 1969 the targa roof Sport Coupe easily outsold the convertible, reversing a preference for open Corvettes which had lasted since 1964. The Coupe now offered the best of both worlds.

A 1969 Tri-power 427 convertible (facing page) with side pipes is definitely one of the great Corvettes and is avidly sought after.

COLORS

Code	Quantity	Body	Suggested interior trim
900	-	Tuxedo Black	Black, Bright Blue, Green, Gunmetal, Red, Saddle
972	-	Can-AmWhite	Black, Bright Blue, Green, Gunmetal, Red, Saddle
974	-	Monza Red	Black, Red, Saddle
976	-	Le Mans Blue	Black, Bright Blue
980	-	Riverside Gold	Black, Saddle
983	-	Fathom Green	Black, Green, Saddle
984	-	Daytona Yellow	Black,
986	-	Cortez Silver	Black, Bright Blue, Green, Gunmetal, Red, Saddle
988	-	Burgundy	Black, Saddle
990	-	Monaco Orange	Black

All wheels were Argent Silver.
Convertible top choice was Black, White or Beige.

the hinge area in the hood surround panel to correct a tendency to cracking at this inside angle, always a weak point with fiberglass construction.

The new Stingray emblems were fixed to the fenders with adhesive and positioned with four locating pins. These fell off or were stolen and a replacement part could be obtained. It has been discovered that some of the replacement emblems had a groove cut below the dot of the letter 'i' of Stingray, leading inevitably to demand for correct replacements. Even these should have the black paint on the wider base of the script only, and not on the raised chromed section.

At the end of 1968 a new factory-fitted TJ2 Front Fender Louver Trim option became available. The four vent grilles behind the front wheel could now be fitted with these optional silver painted and chrome edged metal trims They looked great and made the fourth and rearmost vent, which was a black painted fake, look more convincing. They could be fitted to 1968s too.

From the beginning of 1968 production the black plastic front grilles carried silver paint on the leading edge of their horizontal slats. This paint was discontinued from January 1969, by which time it was already wearing off the cars that had it from new.

January 1969 was also the launch date for the most desirable of all non-engine options and that was the N14 side-mounted exhaust system. Already a proven concept during the three years 1965-67, it followed the same principles established on that earlier model. Two sizes of downpipe were used from the stock cast iron header, 2in for the 350 and 2½in for the 427, these sweeping out behind the front wheel to meet the muffler. While the earlier design had used a chambered pipe as a muffler, the new version used a long oval muffler. The system sounded great, though the charm could diminish on a long trip.

A fluted cast aluminum cover with internal insulation hid the muffler and protected the legs of the occupants when they exited the car on a hot day or after a fast run. Rocker moldings were omitted, and a shaped, black painted upstand on the cover concealed the join between the muffler and the door opening. At the rear under the bumper, a new lower panel was fitted which had no opening for the exhaust, and the rear quarter panel had no cut corresponding cut-out.

Only 4355 1969s were sold new with the side-mounted exhaust, and it was off the option list by the end of the year, but the kit could be bought over the counter and would fit any C3 car. Thousands were sold before supplies of the aluminum covers dried up in 1985, but good old General Motors is still listing the pipes and mufflers 21 years later.

For a correct restoration it is important to establish if sidepipes were originally fitted, and the NCRS has established a useful 8-point test which can be found in the relevant judging manual. This covers the way in which the body was modified on the production line to provide clearance for the system and, just as with the previous model, notes the absence of the rocker molding support tabs, which would otherwise project down from the body birdcage member below the door sill.

The auxiliary hardtop for the convertible continued as for 1968, again with the option of a black vinyl covering, but a useful modification was incorporated after three months of production. Prized possessions though they may be, hardtops inevitably languish in spare rooms or with the yard equipment, so a pair of chrome plated trim tips were thoughtfully provided which not only protected the stylishly flared outer ends of the hardtop but also enabled it to be safely stored with the header rail against a bedroom wall while the tips firmly gripped the carpet. Just to prove that the engineers used these cars themselves, a further improvement was incorporated at the end of the extended 1969 model year with an additional retainer provided below the center of the rear window, allowing an even better fit of the auxiliary top.

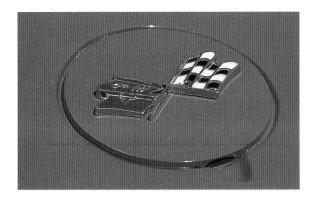

1969 gas filler lid. The filler neck was of 3in diameter, allowing for quick fills in racing pit stops, or more usefully a visual inspection when the fuel gauge was suspect.

The shaped duct on the 427 hood was non-functional and was finished with a pair of chrome and black inserts.

All 1969s carried Stingray emblems. TJ2 Fender Louver Trims looked great and were fitted to far more cars than ever had them originally.

Bumpers were more decorative than protective. The grilles lost their silver leading edges during the 1969 model year.

The N14 Side Mounted Exhaust fitted neatly in place of the rocker panel. It was finished to show car standard and was very loud.

In side view, option N14 side pipes gave the center of the car extra visual muscle. They could get painfully hot, too.

CHASSIS

1969 was the seventh year of production for the faithful Corvette ladder chassis, and the first year for a significant change. To improve the torsional strength of the box-section steel chassis frame, a pair of diagonal braces were added to triangulate the third crossmember to the frame kick-ups. These were effectively behind the lower part of the seat backs, and would be incorporated in all chassis up to 1982. There is no doubt that they worked. No

one would call a 1969 convertible refined, but there is a perceptible improvement over a 1968. Be driven diagonally up a kerb sitting in the passenger's seat with one hand spanning the door and rear fender to feel the difference. In the coupe, the effect is less pronounced because the birdcage built into the separate fiberglass body is also a major contributor to the strength of the whole car.

In April 1968 under-dash reinforcement rods were introduced on convertibles only, to help stiffen these cars. There were three short solid rods

The interior was intimate, and surprisingly tight for such a big car. Bright colors were popular, red being a Corvette tradition since 1953.

Headrests were listed as an option but were fitted to all 1969 Corvettes, as a required option until January 1969 and thereafter as standard equipment.

Sun visors were in Comfort weave to match the interior color.

For 1969 there was a smaller 15in steering wheel, now with a black grained vinyl rim. This is the standard fixed steering column.

For 1969 the seat back latch was moved to half way up the side of the seat for easier access to the luggage compartment.

The optional tilt/telescopic steering column was chosen by a quarter of 1969 buyers. Telescopic action was controlled by rotating lever behind the horn. The tilt lever (far right) was below the turn signal lever. A tilt/telescopic column improves the comfort of any Stingray not already thus equipped.

on the driver's side and two longer tubes under the passenger's dash. These were continued to the end of roadster production in 1975.

INTERIOR

Seats were similar in design to 1968, but the inserts except in very early cars were Comfort-weave, a finer woven material than the 1968 Basket-weave. All 1969 seats were believed to be supplied with head-restraints, initially as a no-choice option and then from January 1 on as standard, fulfilling the requirements of the 1969 Federal Motor Vehicle Safety Standards, which demanded protection against occupant whiplash injuries. When specified, leather was available in a more limited range of colors but in the same pattern as the base seats. All seats 1969-71 had stainless steel seat belt retainers on the lower front of the seat base

The shift console now featured an engine data plate to impress the passenger and flatter the owner, listing the nominal horepower, torque, compression ratio and cubic inch capacity. In front of the passenger there was now an expanding vinyl two-tiered map pocket with one upper and two lower pockets to augment the minimal storage for small personal items.

The door panels were changed to allow slightly more interior space, a panel of Comfort-weave vinyl was added in the recess and a color-matched vertical plastic door pull was provided at the front of the door. This pull was exactly the same part and part number 333535-6 as the 1965 plastic door pull, but used in reverse, so that the left hand carries an 'R'. This part was so flimsy and unsatisfactory that it was replaced in the 1966 Sting Ray by a nice chunky satin chromed pull, part number 3876569-70. Needing a cheap and collapsible handle for the 1969 panel, someone remembered the 1965 unit. The bean counters in the back office must have thrilled at the thought of re-using tooling that had been abandoned after only a year, and this hopeless piece of plastic was revived and fitted to all of the next 300,000 Corvettes made until the end of 1977! The replicas we now buy from the aftermarket are even poorer than the originals - the steel band within the plastic fatigues and snaps - but the 1966-67 satin chrome pulls are still available for $50 a pair and fit straight on.

The new-shaped door panel was still backed with the compressed cellulose board, which ultimately absorbed moisture and lost its shape. Window winders, when fitted, generally had clear plastic knobs except when the interior was black, when they too were black, replacing the co-ordinated knobs of 1968.

The interior lighting was changed in the coupe, perhaps for the worse, by removing the 1968's lights on the interior sail panels and replacing them with just one lamp on the rear wall of the luggage compartment. The coupe rear window storage area now received a black and chrome latch bearing the words 'back window storage'.

INSTRUMENTS & CONTROLS

A new 15in steering wheel with slightly flexible black rim replaced the hard-rimmed fake walnut 16in wheel of the 1968. Better still, the optional N36 telescopic steering column was now replaced by the N37 Tilt-Telescopic column, which was chosen by more than a quarter of buyers. While the telescopic effect of both was to adjust the steering wheel from close to too close, the tilt feature made the reclined seating position much easier to live with. Indeed, for today's enthusiast this is almost an essential, and supply is not such a problem because happily the tilt-telescopic GM Saginaw column is easily adapted to the Corvette from other contemporary GM cars.

The ignition key and cylinder was now moved from the dashboard to a position half way up the right side of the steering column. The cylinder drove a pinion, rack and rod assembly which in turn operated the ignition switch concealed on top of the lower end of the steering column. A cable interlock prevented removal of the square-headed ignition key unless the manual shifter was in reverse or the automatic selector in park, and the gears could not then be shifted unless the lock cylinder was first turned with the correct key, nor could the steering be turned because this was also a steering lock. This was the first serious attempt by General Motors to make their cars harder to steal, and was in response to Federal pressure. The square-headed key also locked the doors, while the oval-head key fitted only the center glovebox compartment lid behind the seats and the spare tire lock.

Instruments and gauges were the same as for the 1968 model, but the radio knobs were changed to a

The manual shift lever was precise and looked great too. A rubber shift boot was used in 1968 and 1969, and the black chrome shift knob was new for 1969.

A black cover plate was fitted to the 777 1969s which were not ordered with a radio.

safety pattern to meet the 1969 FMVSS requirements. The tachometer red lines were the same for each engine option as the 1968 model.

ENGINES

Big news for the 1969 model year was the adoption of the 350 (5.7 liters) to replace the 327 (5.4 liters). This engine size was destined to be powering Corvettes for at least the next 33 years. The extra capacity was achieved by use of a longer 3.48in stroke crankshaft in place of the 327's 3.25in shaft. The base 300hp engine used a nodular iron crank, probably cast number 3932442. Like the one-off 1968 327, the rod journals were of 2.10in diameter and the mains 2.45in. Sensibly, the connecting rod length was once again 5.7in, the longer stroke being accommodated within the piston, which had a shorter pin-to-crown height on the 350.

Base 350 300hp The base 350-300hp engine gained a little more torque over its 327 predecessor with 380lb ft at 3400rpm, and achieved its 300hp at 4800rpm. The engine's air was cleaned by the now classic 14in chrome open-element filter, with decal on the top proclaiming the engine size and power. Beneath was a Rochester Quadrajet 7029202, fitted on cars with automatic transmission or the 720293 four-speed gearbox, and mounted on an orange painted cast iron intake manifold, cast number 3927184. Fuel was delivered to the carburetor with a flow and return system via a two-outlet AC GF432 filter as in 1968.

The oil filler tube on the intake manifold was gone, so oil filling of the engine was now through the orange painted right hand valve cover, as on the big-blocks since 1965. There were two different cylinder heads used during the year, cast numbers 3927186 and 3947041. In the 300hp application, both were fitted with 1.94in intake and 1.50in exhaust valves. Both heads had three tapped bolt holes for the intended direct mounting of the alternator, but for 1969 this was still pivoted on the exhaust manifold. The left hand manifold was cast number 3872765 and had been used on Corvettes since 1966, and the right hand manifold was cast number 3932461 or 3932481. All were tapped for AIR injection fittings

The camshaft for the 300hp was the same as used in 1968 (cast number 3896930), with lift of .390in and a duration of 346° intake and 320° exhaust.

There were three cylinder blocks used during 1969 on both the base 300 and the L46 350 small-block engines. They were cast numbers 3932386, 3956618 and 3970010. This last number was introduced in July 1969, would appear in Corvettes for the next 11 years and is probably the most common small-block engine casting number. All these blocks were fitted with four-bolt main bearing caps in Corvette applications for better restraint of the crankshaft.

Base engine it may have been, but even with the Turbo Hydra-Matic transmission it was good for a 16.0sec standing quarter mile and a top speed of 132mph running a tall 3.08:1 rear axle option. To enjoy a fun, comfortable and reasonably economical vacation in a 1969 Corvette, with some driving on interstates, this engine would be the prime choice.

L46 350 350hp Not available with automatic transmission, this engine continued the tradition and component parts of the 1965 327-350 and was essentially a carryover of the 1968 L79. Just like the 300hp above, the 350hp motor was topped by a 14in chromed air filter and the same intake manifold (cast number 3927184), which supported a Rochester Quadrajet carburetor stamped 7029207.

The cylinder block and cast numbers were exactly as for the 300 horsepower above, while the cylinder head was either cast number 3927186 or 3927187, both with the large 2.02in intake and 1.60in exhaust valves. Bringing back a Corvette tradition established in 1966 was the new version of the aluminum valve cover. Still ribbed, it no longer bore the Corvette script. Instead the left cast aluminum cover had a hole at the front for the PCV fitting, and an oil filler opening to take the chrome-plated twist-in cap at the rear. On the passenger's side the same casting was used but the small hole took the crankcase vent pipe and grommet while the larger boss was shaped to take a cross flag emblem. With typical GM precision a raised square tooth on the boss located in a corresponding slot in the emblem to ensure precise orientation on the assembly line. This cover would remain in use on Corvettes with some color and material variations until the end of C3 production in 1982.

The 350-350's pistons were forged aluminum with an almost rectangular dome and a smaller matching relief for valve clearance. Compression ratio was 11.0:1. The hydraulic camshaft was a new design to go with the larger capacity engine. While retaining the .447in lift of the 1968 327-350, the intake duration was now 346° and the exhaust 340°. The cast number was 3896964, with a vertical diamond.

IDENTIFICATION

Engine block cast numbers

350cu in	3932386, 3932388, 3956618, 397010
427cu in	3935439, 3955270, 3963512
Aluminum ZL1	3946052

Stamped engine number suffixes

HY	350 300hp	Rochester 4BC manual
HZ	350 300hp	Rochester 4BC auto
HW	350 350hp	Rochester 4BC spec high perf, manual
HX	350 350hp	Rochester 4BC spec high perf, manual, AC,
GD	350 350hp	Rochester 4BC spec high perf, manual, AC, K66
LM	427 390hp	Rochester 4BC, hydr. lifters, manual
LL	427 390hp	Rochester 4BC, hydr. lifters, auto
MH	427 390hp	Rochester 4BC, hydr. lifters, manual, K66
MI	427 390hp	Rochester 4BC, hydr. lifters, auto, K66
LQ	427 400hp	Holley 3x2BC, hydr. lifters, manual
LN	427 400hp	Holley 3x2BC, hydr. lifters, auto
MJ	427 400hp	Holley 3x2BC, hydr. lifters, auto, K66
MK	427 400hp	Holley 3x2BC, hydr. lifters, manual, K66
LR	427 435hp	Holley 3x2BC, mech. lifters, manual
LT	427 435hp	Holley 3x2BC, mech. lifters, manual, dual plate clutch
LX	427 435hp	Holley 3x2BC, mech. lifters, auto
LP	427 435hp	L89. Holley 3x2BC, mech. lifters, manual, alloy heads
LW	427 435hp	L89. Holley 3x2BC, mech. lifters, auto, alloy heads
LU	427 435hp	L89. Holley 3x2BC, mech. lifters, manual, alloy heads, dual plate clutch
LO	427 430hp	L88.Holley 4BC, mech. lifters, M22 manual (560bhp)
LV	427 430hp	L88.Holley 4BC, mech. lifters, M22 manual (560bhp)
MR	427 430hp	L88.Holley 4BC, mech. lifters, M22 manual, K66 (560bhp)
ME	427 430hp	ZL1. Alloy block, Holley 4BC, mech lifters, M22 manual
MG	427 430hp	ZL1. Alloy block, Holley 4BC, mech lifters, auto
MS	427	Use unknown

Chassis numbers
194379S3700001 through 194379S738762
(4th digit for a convertible is 6)

Exhaust manifolds were the same as the for the base engine, with a 2in outlet, and like the 300hp small-blocks this one used 2in exhaust pipes too. As in 1968, all engines came equipped with AIR systems. The air injection pump for 1969 was a 7805650.

L36 427 390hp Five of the 1969 big-block engines were direct carryovers from 1968. There were three block casting numbers used. The first, 3935439, was used on '69 models until the end of December 1968 and was also used on late '68s. The second was the rare 3955270 and ran for just half of the month January 1969, having been produced for only about two months in the fall of 1968. The third big-block crankcase (cast number 3963512) was then used until the end of 1971. It was modified to accept the longer throw of the 454 and was used for both sizes of engine. There was an additional ZL1 aluminum option, described fully at the end of this section.

Beneath the 14in chromed air filter on the base L36 big-block sat the Rochester Quadrajet, numbered 7028209 for the four-speed or 7028216 for the Turbo Hydra-Matic 400. Like all 427s for this year, the intake manifold was weight-saving and better looking aluminum, though the effect was marred by the intrusive AIR pump.

Cylinder heads were cast number 3931063, with

2.06in intake and 1.72in exhaust valves, set off with chrome-plated stamped steel valve covers. The camshaft was the same as for the 1968 engine but was now cast number 3883944. The forged pistons were domed with a small valve relief, and gave a compression of 10.25:1.

With torque of 460lb ft at only 3600rpm the L36 427-390 had the ability to pull a 3.08 axle with the four-speed Muncie or a super-tall 2.73 ratio with the Turbo Hydra-Matic 400. This ability, combined with the appeal of the simple and reliable Rochester

L36 390hp (above) was the most tractable of the 427 big-blocks. The Holley carburetor was mounted on an aluminum intake manifold and the motor ran hydraulic lifters. The Air Injection Reactor (AIR) pump (left) promoted a secondary burn in the exhaust system and didn't use much power, but it growled and whistled and was usually removed when its inadequate bearings expired.

L68 400hp was the same as the 390hp but three two-barrel Holleys replaced the single four-barrel.

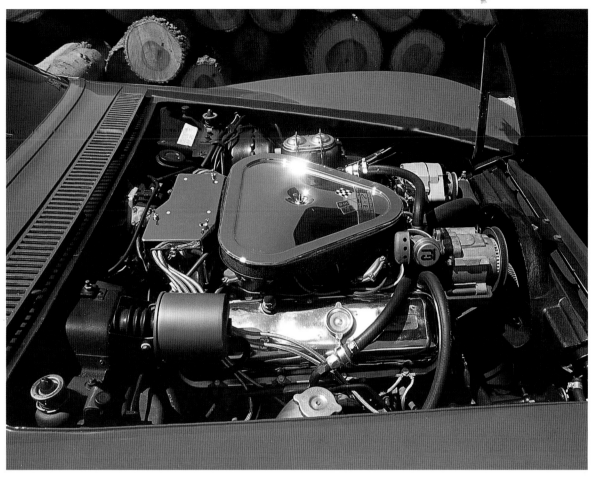

Dramatic triangular Tri-Power air cleaner had an oiled foam filter element.

Quadrajet, make it a very tempting engine for today's enthusiast.

L68 427 400hp Just as in 1968, the L68 gained ten horsepower over the L36 by simply substituting the four venturi of the Quadrajet with the six venturi of a Tri-Power Holley on a special manifold. For fuller information, see the previous chapter. For 1969 the front and rear two-barrel Holley 3659 carbs were stamped 3902353. The center unit was 3940929 for the four-speed and 3940930 for the automatic. The aluminum intake manifold was cast number 3937795, as found on late 1968s.

L71 427 435hp Again this solid-lifter high-performance version of the Tri-Power was a carry over from 1968. The cast 3937797 intake manifold, 3919840 big-valve cylinder heads, and the 3880827 and 3880828 exhaust manifolds were all identical too. For more details see previous chapter. This was the last year for the Tri-Power.

L89 427 435hp Identical to the L71, this rare option was achieved by fitting the 3919842 aluminum cylinder heads to the L71, just as in 1968. Only 390 cars were thus equipped, so this is an even rarer option than in 1968 when 624 were built. Because a 1969 is more desirable than a 1968

Triple two-barrels needed careful set-up and regular use. Front and rear throttles were vacuum controlled. Ten horsepower was gained by better mixture distribution.

- wider wheels, better steering column and wheel – then this is the easiest high–dollar car to counterfeit. You need someone to attest that your L89 is genuine – don't ask this author!

L88 427 430hp Probably developing a true 550hp at 6400rpm, the L88 was the craziest 427 ever, and 1969 was the last year for the ultimate expression of Corvette mass-production big-block power. For this year only it was even available with the Turbo Hydra-Matic 400, reflecting the importance of drag racing at that time.

The L88 was fitted with the new open chamber design aluminum cylinder head, cast number 3946074. The earlier big-block heads, now called closed chamber, had a kidney profile when viewed at the mating face. On the new open chamber head the squish area around the spark plug was cut away, reducing the compression ratio but more than compensating for this by improved gas flow. This head also had a round exhaust port, and slightly bigger exhaust valves, increased to 1.88in from 1.72in. A big 850cfm Holley R4296 stamped 3955205 fed a tall aluminum 3933198 intake manifold, and the same carburetor was also used on the rare automatics. An improved forged steel connecting rod with thicker beam now carried $^{7}/_{16}$in rod bolts with ground shanks.

None of the previous L88s since 1967 had been fitted with shrouds on their aluminum radiators but all were manual transmission cars. To allow for

Big-block radio interference protection was limited to a distributor shield and stainless steel sheaths for the plug wires, which were grounded at each end.

cooling of the 400 automatic in the L88, a copper radiator was fitted together with a fiberglass shroud.

ZL1 427 aluminum block This car probably has no place in a book about production Corvettes. In more than 30 years only one ZL1 has been positively identified as genuine, so that really makes it a prototype or one-off factory special. On the other hand this one car has had such a strange history and been so much copied that it would be wrong to omit it. GM figures appear to show that two actual production cars were built but the whereabouts of the second ZL1 is unknown, even if there really was one. Additionally it is known that two 1968 roadsters and one 1969 prototype were built and shown to the press.

There is a club for ZL1 owners and the members are almost all Camaro drivers. We

This L88 is one of only 17 produced with automatic transmission. Most were ordered to be raced, and few would have retained their stock wheels or optional whitewalls for long.

usually forget that most Corvette engines of this period were also available in the F-body Chevrolet, so why should it matter when a Camaro engine is fitted to a Corvette? The answer is that Chevrolet put 69 of their lightweight monster motors into the Camaro but only fitted one or two into the Corvette.

The ZL1 was essentially an L88 with an aluminum block in lieu of cast iron. The block was cast number 3946052 and was fitted with steel liners. It was the same block that powered the awesome Can-Am championship winning McLaren M8As to first and second place driven by Bruce McLaren and Denny Hulme. It weighed about 200lb less than its

cast iron sister, and about 30lb less than a small-block. The block itself was about 100lb lighter than its cast iron sister. When it was shown to the press in March 1969, Zora Arkus-Duntov was asked what kind of person would buy a ZL1. In his characteristic strong middle European accent he replied, 'First, he'll have a lot money.' The ZL1 option cost $3000 more than the L88.

It was more powerful than the L88, on which it was broadly based, with figures of up to 580hp suggested. The 3946074 cylinder heads carried extra bolt holes which located into new bosses in the valley of the block in an attempt to hold the engine together. The camshaft duration was the same as the L88, but the valve lift was now an incredible .579in intake and .584in exhaust. The pistons had big domes and yielded a 12.5:1 compression ratio. The engine was well suited to the Camaro, which was doing particularly well in circuit racing at the time, Mark Donahue and Roger Penske winning the SCCA Trans-Am championship in 1969. Lighter than the Corvette and with its engine weight further forward, the Camaro stood to benefit much more than the Corvette from the weight saving potential. In fact, 50 of the 69 ZL1-engined Camaros were actually ordered by one dealer for NHRA drag racing

under a Central Office Production Order (COPO), number 9561. The ZL1 Corvette was never apparently advertised, nor did it appear as an option in the 1969 catalogs. However, it was shown as regular production option RPO ZL1 in Chevrolet's end-of-year production report, and further that report stated that two were built.

Every Corvette has an interesting history, but the ZL1 VIN 194379S729219 is extraordinary, and has been well researched by Rick Bizzoco for his indispensable *1969 Stingray Guidebook*. He reports that the Daytona Yellow ZL1 was originally ordered by the Plant Resident Engineer at the St Louis Corvette assembly plant in July 1969, as his company car. It was built on September 11 and the engineer used it for some 2000 miles before he was transferred to another vehicle. The car stayed at the plant. It was then sent to Hechler Chevrolet in Richmond, Virginia, where it was offered for sale, probably as an ex-factory demonstrator, at virtually the list price of $10,773.65 in December 1969. This was more than double the $4438 cost of a basic 1969 coupe. The car was displayed in the showroom next to a similarly engined ZL1 Camaro, and it was finally sold on January 20 1970 to John Zagos, a drag boat racer, for a much reduced $8100. He dropped a valve in the motor by over-revving it

The awesome L88, cataloged at 430hp, probably developed a true 550 horsepower. The air cleaner was concealed in the special cold air induction hood.

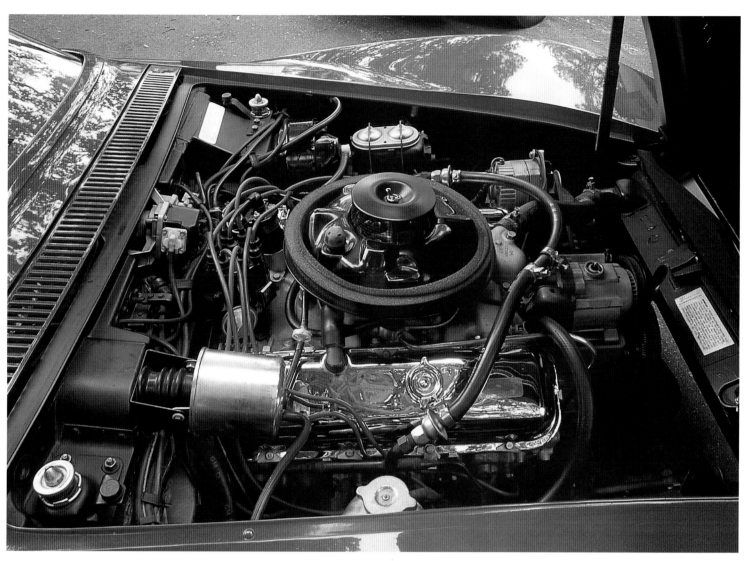

With no radio, the L88 had no ignition shielding, but like all 1969s it still had an AIR pump. Perhaps to discourage street use, no fan or radiator shroud was fitted to the L88. The L88's 12.5:1 compression ratio required special gasoline (right).

on the first night of ownership, persuaded a full replacement motor out of Chevrolet under his 12 month/12,000 mile warranty - offering to fit the motor himself - and happily failed to return the core as well! He never fitted the replacement ZL1 either and eventually sold the car back to Hechler Chevrolet with a standard passenger-car 454 engine installed, and it was sold on.

Wayne Walker of the well-known Corvette parts specialist Zip Products then bought the car in November 1976 and within a few months he had located the original engine. I saw the restored

chassis which he displayed at the Knoxville, Tennessee, Corvette Expo show in 1980 (but was more interested in the low-mileage 1970 LT1 that I bought there for myself). The body was restored and refitted and the finished car appeared on the cover of his Zip Corvette parts catalog in 1983. He sold the car to enthusiast Ed Mueller in 1986, who showed it at the Cypress Gardens FL and Bloomington Gold IL events. Mueller then sold the car in 1989 to Craig Priest, a dealer in Miami, who showed it again at Cypress Gardens and then sold it to Richard Lynn of Florida. According to USA Today of October 1991, federal agents then seized the car from Lynn after he was convicted in 1989 of smuggling 3300lb of cocaine between 1985 and 1988, and the car was forfeit.

So the extraordinary situation arose where the federal government, which had spent the previous 20 years forcing fuel economy, speed restriction, safety and environmental controls on the American automobile, at last had in its possession one of the fastest, thirstiest and most anti-social cars ever built. Happily for us, it passed up the opportunity to crush the car and teach us all a lesson, and instead decided it was to be auctioned, the proceeds sensibly going to anti-drug abuse programs in Alabama, where Lynn had been operating. At a GSA auction at the

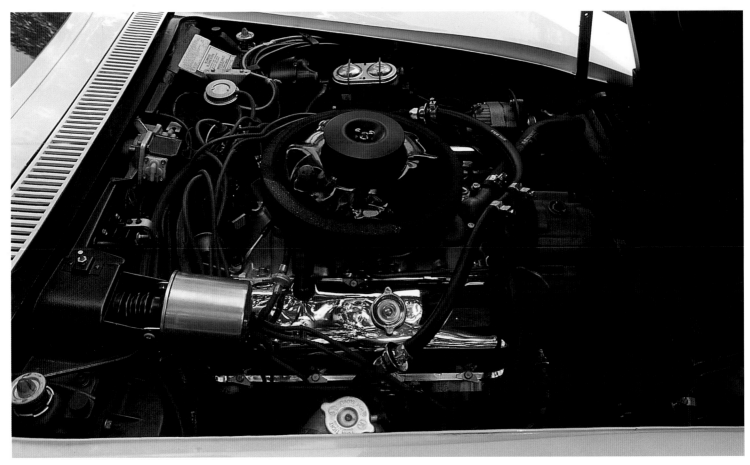

This L88 is one of only 17 produced with Turbo Hydra-Matic transmission. All of these cars were believed to have been equipped with a radiator shroud.

Kennedy Space Center on October 12 1991 it was bought for an alleged $300,000 by Roger Judski, the well-known Corvette dealer of Maitland, Florida.

If you wanted to build yourself a replica ZL1 today, you could do it in a matter of weeks and for a fraction of the value of the original car. You would need a good used 1969 427 four-speed coupe, a set of heavy-duty 2-pin caliper brakes, a pair of 3946074 aluminum heads, a 198 intake open plenum intake manifold (widely offered at swap meets), a new 4296 Holley 850cfm double pumper and a good set of N14 side-mount exhausts. GM still periodically sell the aluminum cylinder block, so you would need a good engine builder to assemble and dyno test it. You would also need to change the hood for a cold air L-88 style replica, widely available, and then have the car striped with the unique ZL1 broad decal which stretches over the front fender peaks, using the detailed drawings in the 1969 Assembly Instruction Manual. Apart from the paperwork and build sheet, and the wrong numbers on the block, you would have a car exactly like that most widely desired and famous Shark of them all.

COOLING SYSTEM

The radiator choice in 1969, aluminum or copper, was determined by engine and transmission options and whether air conditioning was fitted. In effect all small-block cars used an aluminum radiator unless they had either the Turbo Hydra-Matic 400 or air conditioning, whle all big-block cars used a copper radiator except the manual L-88. The expansion tank was either aluminum or the long thin brass tank. The small-block engines used the aluminum tank unless they had air conditioning, and the big-block cars all used the aluminum tank unless they had air conditioning, in which case they used the long copper tank.

ELECTRICS

To anyone who sells old Corvettes to earn a living, the single most disliked feature of the 1968-82 model must be the battery location in the compartment behind the driver's seat.

To struggle on a cold day connecting heavy-duty jumper wires to those inaccessible terminals, and then to try to sit a tall body in the seat to press the clutch without displacing the clips was difficult enough, but then Chevrolet made things even harder from June 1969 when they introduced the first side-terminal battery. Not surprisingly, many owners solve the problem by using the door striker as an alternative connection for the ground wire, though this is not recommended. To be fair the side-terminal battery was invented to solve the

Headlamp washers were new for 1969. Twin nozzles washed the low beams whenever the screen washer was used.

Fiber-optics monitored the rear lamps. Panel listed horsepower, torque, engine capacity and compression ratio.

The rear appearance was simplified, and costs saved, by using the inner rear lamps for back-up lights.

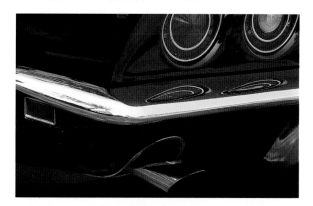

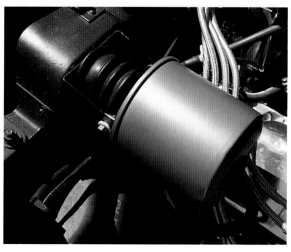

The vacuum canister for lifting the wiper flap – this changed to a more compact design late in 1969.

problem of corrosion on battery terminals, and in this it was completely successful.

For 1969 the side marker lights now used amber plastic lenses instead of the clear lens and amber bulb of 1968, while the rear lenses continued in red. More interestingly, the headlights were now fitted with washers. Certainly a first for an American production car, they were teed off the main washer system and washed the outer of the pairs of lamps whenever the windshield washer button was pressed. While this emptied the small washer bottle twice as quickly as before, it was an impressive talking point, but it was quietly dropped within two years, never to be seen again on a Corvette. Let us assume that unlike Volvo and Saab owners whose washers are so obvious, Corvette drivers do not tailgate the car they are following on wet nights and thus keep their headlights clean anyway!

An optional audio alarm which appeared on a few late 1968 cars became a popular option for 1969, sounding the horn when set if the doors or hood were opened. It was key operated with a lock mounted in the rear panel. By modern standards it is a hopeless deterrent, but its presence may have saved owners thousands of dollars in insurance premiums.

TRANSMISSIONS

The rare three-speed transmission continued as the base option for the 1969 for the last time, with only about 250 cars sold with it. Almost all of those will have been retro-fitted with a four-speed. The 1969 manual Muncie transmission had a modified shift lever fixing on the side cover, which now used a bolt into a threaded hole rather than a nut and locking washer.

WHEELS & TIRES

The shark body came of age and looked just right when it finally got its 8in wide wheels in 1969. The tire size was unchanged, so it is hard to know why the 7in wheel was used through 1968. This was the age of the custom wheel anyway, so Rally wheels were discarded wholesale and Cragar, American and Halibrand wheels replaced them, often with extended wheel arches too.

The standard hub cap and trim were the same as for 1968 and would continue for another 14 years. The optional P01 full wheelcover of 1968 was now renamed a P02 De Luxe wheelcover for 1969 and was introduced late in the 1968 production run. The design was slightly different, with a second ring around the center cap which made it look less obtrusive.

Tire choice for 1969 was initially the same as for 1968, but at the end of the summer of 1969 the

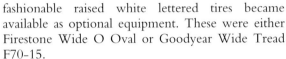

AM/FM radio (far left) was available in mono or stereo. The design was unique to the Corvette. The Rally wheel (left) was now a full 8in wide. This two-piece center cap and trim ring combination would run for an unprecedented 15 years, and it still looks great.

fashionable raised white lettered tires became available as optional equipment. These were either Firestone Wide O Oval or Goodyear Wide Tread F70-15.

SUSPENSION & STEERING

The suspension was almost the same as in 1968 apart from one small but significant change to the steering knuckle. The front wheel spindle was enlarged so that it now took a pair of larger bearings, retained by a larger $^{27}\!/_{32}$in x 20tpi nut. Since 1963 the front spindle nut had been the same ½in as the rear. It would be nice but wrong to assume that this was a move on the part of the Corvette engineering team led by Zora Arkus-Duntov to upgrade the car. The truth was that the full-size Impala sedan was getting heavier, at up to 4300lb for a station wagon, and needed a stronger knuckle. The company made more than 1,000,000 1969 full-size Chevrolets and just 38,762 Corvettes. They shared this component so the 3100lb sports car benefited.

The optional F41 heav-duty suspension used stiffer and shorter front springs and shocks, as previously. The standard rear suspension used the nine-leaf transverse spring, while the F41 used a stiffer seven-leaf. The rear sway bar was of ⅝in diameter and fitted to all big-blocks and F41 optioned cars.

BRAKES

The brakes were a direct carry-over from 1968, with the J50 power brakes adding a vacuum booster and J56 option Special Heavy Duty Brakes. This was the last year for J56, but the special caliper and pad combination would reappear in the 'Z' series options from 1971 to 1975.

	OPTIONS		
Code	Option	Quantity	Price
19437	Base Corvette Sport Coupe	22129	$4781.00
19467	Base Corvette Convertible	16633	$4438.00
ZQ3	Base 350 300hp motor	10083	$0.00
	Base three-speed	252	$0.00
	Base vinyl trim	35033	$0.00
	Leather seats	3729	$79.00
A01	Soft Ray tinted glass	31270	$16.90
A31	Power windows	9816	$63.20
A82	Headrests, mandatory	38762	$17.95
A85	Shoulder harness, std with coupe	600	$42.15
C07	Auxiliary hardtop (19467 only)	7878	$252.80
C08	Auxiliary top exterior vinyl trim	3266	$57.95
C50	Rear window defroster	2485	$32.65
C60	Air conditioning	11959	$428.70
F41	Special front & rear suspension	1661	$36.90
G81	Positraction rear axle, all ratios	36965	$46.35
J50	Power brakes	16876	$42.15
J56	Heavy duty brakes	115	$384.45
K66	Transistor ignition	5702	$81.10
KO5	Engine block heater	824	$10.55
L36	427 390hp engine	10531	$221.20
L46	350 350hp engine	12846	$131.65
L68	427 400hp engine	2072	$326.55
L71	427 435hp engine	2722	$437.10
L88	427 430hp engine	116	$1,032.15
L89	L71 with aluminum heads 435hp	390	$832.05
MA6	Twin plate clutch	102	$79.00
M20	Four-speed manual wide ratio	16507	$184.80
M21	Four-speed manual close ratio	13741	$184.80
M22	Four-speed manual heavy duty	101	$290.42
M40	Turbo Hydra-Matic transmission	8161	$221.80
N14	Side mounted exhaust	4355	$147.45
N37	Tilt/telescopic steering column	10325	$84.30
N40	Power-assisted steering	22866	$105.35
P02	Full wheelcovers	8073	$57.95
PT6	Red stripe tires F70 x15	5210	$31.30
PT7	White stripe tires F70 x 15	21379	$31.30
PU9	White letter tires F70 x 15	2398	$33.15
TJ2	Front fender louver trim	11962	$21.10
UA6	Alarm system	12436	$26.35
U15	Speed warning indicator	3561	$11.60
U69	AM/FM radio	33871	$172.75
U79	Stereo AM/FM radio	4114	$278.10
ZL1	Special aluminum motor	2	$3,000.00

1970-72

The targa-roof coupe outsold the convertible by more than two to one over the three years 1970-72. Darker metallic colors such as Brands Hatch Green and this Laguna Gray were very popular in the early 1970s.

Many enthusiasts believe that 1970 saw the beginning of a golden age of Corvette design, an age that ended with the last chrome front bumper in July of 1972. Thereafter the intrusive hand of government would be felt in the design of all cars sold in the United States, and the first impact would strike the front bumper of the Corvette the following model year. Never before would legislation have such a profound effect on the styling of the nation's cars.

It was a golden age that had a very late start. Back then, the United Auto Workers union, UAW, performed a ritual dance with General Motors, Ford and Chrysler in which they walked out on strike on one of these Big Three every year. Workers at the other two giants stayed working while the strikers struck on their behalf. However, a strike against St Louis and other Chevrolet plants during the spring of 1969 was not part of this round but related to other issues including the ultimately unhappy establishment of the General Motors Assembly Division. Where previously each division built its own cars, sometimes with Fisher, GMAD would now build

all GM cars, leaving the five brands as marketing organizations. The dispute prevented production of cars between April 10 and June 9 1969. This eight-week shutdown meant that there were not only many unfilled orders, but parts had already been ordered and made which would not carry over into a new model year. The model changeover, which normally happened in August, was therefore delayed to January 1970.

So the final production total for 1970 was just 17,316, not helped by a strike of Teamsters Union truck drivers and associated workers from April 6 to May 6 which shut down the lines again due to shortage of parts. In the fall of 1970 it was GM's turn for the national strike, which lasted from September 15 through November 24, again reducing Corvette production, to just 21,801 for the 1971 model year.

In most aspects the 1971 was a continuation of 1970, the majority of changes occurring for the 1972 model year. In particular the VIN number changed to incorporate the engine option as the fifth digit. For 1972 these were K for the base 200hp 350, L for the 255hp LT1 350 and W for the 454.

DIMENSIONS & WEIGHTS

Length	182.5in
Width	69.2in
Height	
Sport Coupe	47.75in
Convertible	47.8in
Wheelbase	98.0in
Max track	
Front	58.7in
Rear	59.4in
Curb weight	
Sport Coupe	3285lb
Convertible	3300lb

The combative attitude between management and unions, particularly in the early 1970s, did nothing to improve quality and gave away much of the market to oriental imports. That the Corvette was able to survive that competition speaks much for its fundamental appeal, and while the imports were quieter, better built and nimbler, no competitor offered anything like the power, rugged construction or sheer brute appeal of the Corvette.

In many years of buying, selling, servicing and driving chrome bumpered Shark shaped Corvettes, I have generally found that the 1970-72 cars feel and drive better than 1969s, which in turn are almost always better than 1968s. While they are essentially the same cars, there were many minor detailed improvements which, along with the better seats, just make them tighter and more satisfying to drive.

BODY & BODY TRIM

Perhaps knowing that they were even then enjoying the last days of aggressive front end metalwork, the stylists removed the cheap plastic grilles, utilitarian parking lamps and separate lower moldings and replaced them with a magnificent pair of chromed diecast grilles which incorporated both the lower trims and shapely new parking lamps. The grille was a masterly demonstration of what Detroit then did so well, a superb casting in which the multiple square grille appertures were finished in satin gray, emphasising the bright finish on the front. The vertical front bumperettes were reshaped to fit the new grilles too.

Slight flares at the back of each wheel opening protected the body sides from wheel spray without detracting from the pure form of the body.

	COLORS 1970		
Code	**Quantity**	**Body**	**Suggested interior trim**
972	-	Classic White	Blue, Black, Brown, Green, Red, Saddle
974	-	Monza Red.	Black, Brown, Red, Saddle
975	-	Malboro Maroon	Black, Brown, Saddle
976	-	Mulsanne Blue	Blue, Black
979	-	Bridgehampton Blue	Blue, Black
982	-	Donnybrooke Green	Black, Brown, Green, Saddle
984	-	Daytona Yellow	Black, Green
986	-	Cortez Silver	Black, Blue, Brown, Green, Red, Saddle
991	-	Ontario Orange	Black, Saddle
992	-	Laguna Gray	Black, Blue, Brown, Green, Red, Saddle
993	-	Corvette Bronze	Black

All wheels were Argent Silver. Convertible top choice was Black, White or Beige. Custom leather interior was Black or Saddle only.

The elemental sports car. Big engine, four big wheels and just two seats, with no room for anyone or anything extra.

The new diecast metal grilles for air inlet and outlet were subtly chrome edged. Of course most of the cooling air entered the intake below the grilles.

Over the production period there were three different grilles made. The first was used for all of 1970 and for the first 1450 cars of 1971. Then two holes for fixing screws appeared on the lower edge of the grille, replacing previously hidden and troublesome fixing studs. In June 1971, the hole for the fiber optic socket in the top of the parking lamp was deleted when the failure alert system for the parking lamp was discontinued early for the 1972 model year. There was always a single screw hole at the outer edge of the outer molding, and the service parts from GM have all three holes as used in 1971. The parking lamp lenses were clear plastic with an amber bulb, but in 1972 the lens material was changed to amber and a clear bulb was used instead.

The side marker lamps increased in size and, rather than being recessed at an angle, the larger amber lens front marker lamps were trapezium shaped and set flush with the body. The rear marker lamps were larger too and both had diecast metal bodies.

The other major external change to the body for 1970 was to treat the four wheel openings with extensions to act as mud deflectors – sounded terrible but looked great. The 8in wheels of the 1969 had thrown up more road dirt than the 7in wheels of the 1968 so it was logical do something about the rooster-tails of mud printed on the sides

of the car. After all, this was an all-weather car with non-rusting bodywork and there was no reason to leave it at home when the roads were wet. GM styling were masters of the impossible - they put spoilers on the front of each wheel opening on the Pontiac Trans-Am and made them look great - and the work on the Corvette was no less successful. It didn't keep the sides of the car clean, but it lowered the tide mark.

Perhaps the most obvious and effective change to the body was the new front fender air vents. These were given new cast outlet grilles in the style of the

A new aluminum rocker trim emphasized the waisted Coke bottle profile. The side exhaust was no longer available, having been a 1969-only option, but it remained a popular retro-fit.

COLORS 1971

Code	Quantity	Body	Suggested interior trim
905	1177	Nevada Silver	Black, Dark Blue, Dark Green, Red
912	1177	Sunflower Yellow	Black, Dark Green, Saddle
972	1875	Classic White	Black, Dark Blue, Dark Green, Red, Saddle
973	2180	Mille Miglia Red.	Black, Red
976	2465	Mulsanne Blue	Black, Dark Blue
979	1417	Bridgehampton Blue	Black, Dark Blue
983	3445	Brands Hatch Green	Black, Dark Green
987	2269	Ontario Orange	Black, Dark Green, Saddle
988	1591	Steel Cities Gray	Black, Saddle
989	3706	War Bonnet Yellow	Black, Dark Green, Saddle

All wheels were Argent Silver. Convertible top choice was Black or White. Custom leather interior was Black or Saddle only.

The Kamm-type tail with its vestigial spoiler reduced rear drag, but overall the drag coefficient of the car was not exceptionally good.

Roof up, the convertible top was trim, taut and an inch lower than the coupe roof. Rear visibility was better than today's C5 too.

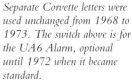

Separate Corvette letters were used unchanged from 1968 to 1973. The switch above is for the UA6 Alarm, optional until 1972 when it became standard.

As on all Corvette convertibles from 1963 to 1990, the top could be lowered and stowed by the driver alone while remaining seated – very useful at traffic lights. Since 1990 the deck release switch has been behind the driver's left shoulder, preventing this impressive performance unless the switch is relocated. Redesigned for 1969, the concealed door handle (below) was used for the next 14 years.

front intakes, aping the Mercedes 300SL of the 1950s but more importantly giving a more horizontal and sleek emphasis to the side of the car. They were painted body color, with the chromed pattern subtly exposed. On cars up to the first few weeks of 1971 production, the chrome was exposed only on the horizontals. Thereafter, the casting was changed to emphasise the verticals more and these too were now exposed, making a squared pattern of chrome. Interestingly, NCRS research suggests that the chrome was not masked on some silver and gray cars, as though the effect on these colors did not justify the effort of masking.

Between the wheels, the two-piece fiberglass and aluminum rocker molding assembly was replaced by a single aluminum trim, covering the otherwise exposed frame side rail. This part, like so many on the Stingray, was destined for another 12 years of service. The dramatic side exhaust had been discontinued at the end of the 1969 model year, although it could still be bought and fitted as an over-the-counter part. To compensate for the lack of a side exhaust option for 1970, two great looking

new rectangular rear exhaust outlets emphasised the power and purpose of the car. They were made of chrome-plated steel, and rusted quickly, but stainless reproductions were soon on the market. These were framed in turn by chromed diecast bezels on the lower rear panel.

The gas filler lid for 1970 used the same nylon closure latch as the 1969, but for 1971 an over-

COLORS 1972

Code	Quantity	Body	Suggested interior trim
912	1543	Sunflower Yellow	Black, Saddle
924	1372	Pewter Silver	Blue, Black, Red, Saddle
945	1617	Briar Blue,	Black
946	4200	Elkhart Green	Black, Saddle
972	2763	Classic White	Blue, Black, Red, Saddle
973	2478	Mille Miglia Red.	Black, Red, Saddle
979	3198	Targa Blue	Blue, Black
987	4891	Ontario Orange	Black, Saddle
988	2346	Steel Cities Gray	Black, Red, Saddle
989	2550	War Bonnet Yellow	Black, Saddle

All wheels were Argent Silver. Convertible top choice was Black or White. Custom leather interior was Black or Saddle only.

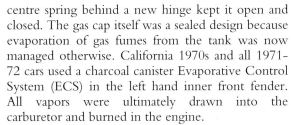

centre spring behind a new hinge kept it open and closed. The gas cap itself was a sealed design because evaporation of gas fumes from the tank was now managed otherwise. California 1970s and all 1971-72 cars used a charcoal canister Evaporative Control System (ECS) in the left hand inner front fender. All vapors were ultimately drawn into the carburetor and burned in the engine.

Other changes were more subtle. All cars now had tinted glass. The new 1970 colors were much improved, while Black, a staple almost every year since 1954, was unavailable and would not reappear for another seven years. These were times for subtle metallic shades. Though no figures are available for colors for 1969 or 1970, we know that in 1968 and 1971 the most popular colors were British Green and Brands Hatch Green respectively. Surprisingly too, Red was never the most popular color for any of the years 1968-82. Indeed, the most popular color for the all C3 production by a big margin is technically not a color at all – White!

While there were subtle changes in the center mounting bracket during the five years of production the front bumper is effectively the same from 1968 to 1972.

CHASSIS

Having been reinforced with new diagonals at the frame kick-ups and other areas in 1969, the frame was continued virtually unchanged from 1970 to 1972 and the new frames now available fit 1969 through 1974. The frame for automatic transmission cars was still made with a removable crossmember

INTERIOR

1970 saw some effective re-design of the interior which would run for virtually eight years. There were new seats, taller and better shaped, with no separate head restraint. The backrest release was moved to the top back of the seat, so hingeing the seat back to load the luggage area was now a single-handed task. A shoulder-level trim piece accommodated the shoulder belt, standard on coupes and optional on the convertible. Vinyl seats for all three years were stitched with longitudinal panels. The door panels were revised and slimmed again, and were finished with a deep metal trim along the

With the rear window removed and stowed in its own compartment beneath the rear deck (above), the t-roof coupe was almost a convertible. This was not lost on buyers, who ordered far more of the coupes, hastening the demise of the soft top at the end of 1975 production, not to resume until 1986. Rectangular exhaust trim (right) with matching body bezel was pure GM Styling Section at its best.

The muffler was always a tight fit between the spare wheel carrier and the rear fender. When new, the intermediate exhaust pipe was welded to the muffler as a one-piece unit. These are now available again.

Nose and gas lid emblems were the familiar Chevrolet flag crossed with winner's checkered flag. The Chevrolet flag combined the Chevrolet Bowtie with the Fleur de Lys, associated with the French but originally a Greek symbol of virility.

Wide door had close-spaced hinges (far left) which were stressed and prone to wear but happily they had bronze bushes which could easily be replaced. The carpeted kick area and the chrome divider have been added by the owner on this car. A base door panel (left) in Saddle, with power windows.

With the soft-top neatly stowed under the deck lid, the convertible's interior was particularly inviting. Steep windshield gave excellent protection.

Headlight switch controlled vacuum actuators too, and rotated for cluster dimming and interior lights.

middle of the panel. Loop carpet was established as the base trim in this year.

A new de luxe interior was introduced, Custom Interior Trim now replacing the previous two years' Genuine Leather Seats. The new package included leather seats and more luxurious cut pile carpet but was only available in Black or Saddle. This was a cutback on 1969 when a range of colors were available in leather, and the restricted choice continued through 1972. The stitched panels of the leather seats for 1970 and half of 1971 were longitudinal, as on the vinyl seats, but changed to transverse for the rest of the this period and through 1974 too. Today, vendors offer the full of range colors in leather and it is hard indeed to restore, say, a 1972 red interior and not give oneself leather to sit on. After tens of thousands of miles sitting on Comfort-weave vinyl I can attest that the name is an oxymoron.

Beige interior should be in Comfort-weave as leather was originally available only in the darker Saddle or in Black for 1970-72. Leather looks great though.

Left pull switch raised the headlamp pods only, right raised the wiper cover only. The central knob rotated to cut power to the wipers, enabling blades to be changed.

Ever since it adorned the first 300 1953 Corvettes, Red has always been a popular interior color, but it was available only in vinyl for 1970-1972, so this is a replacement. The wiper switch (below) offered two speeds and is pushed to operate the screen and headlamp washers. The Corvette emblem appeared here only on cars without air conditioning.

Taller seats with integral head rests were a real improvement over 1968 and 1969. The seat back release button was logically behind the head rest, a spring steel strip restrained the seat, and rake was adjusted at these buffers (right). On coupes the shoulder belt passed through a black trim panel (far right). Lap belts only were fitted to convertibles, unless the shoulder belt was ordered as option A85.

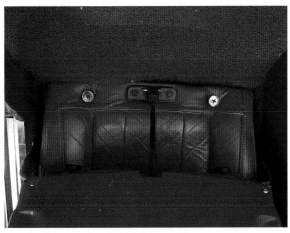

The four-speed shifter (above) on the Muncie had a reverse lock-out and a black chrome ball. The parking brake lever (right) controlled a weak emergency brake system.

The Custom Interior Trim also included cut pile carpet fitted on the bottoms of the door panels, neatly finished with a curved chromed separator trim, and the middle door trim was decorated with a material never previously exposed on a Corvette except on optional steering wheels – wood, a veneer believed to be walnut. The gearshift console was trimmed to match with a thin veneer of the same material.

INSTRUMENTS & CONTROLS

The changes introduced in 1969 were carried on through 1972. The pedals had the bright stainless steel trims through the end of 1971 production, when they were discontinued. The same brake and clutch pedal rubbers were used without the trims for 1972, when a smaller accelerator pedal was fitted.

ENGINES

The steering wheel was unchanged but the horn button was rich in decorative significance to those in pursuit of absolute originality. The right hand of the two Corvette crossed flags was chequered. On the 1970 and 1972 cars the top right hand square of this flag was black, while on the 1971 it was white. If this all sounds familiar, there was a similar variation in gas cap emblems on 1966 Corvettes!

All the instruments had green lettering on a black background until 1972, when the lettering was changed to white. Needles were all red.

The seat belt warning lamp button continued to require a manual reset each time the engine was started through the end of 1971 production. In early 1972 this changed to a light and buzzer controlled by a 15-second timer. Later in the model year the lamp was lit and the buzzer sounded until the seat belt was pulled out, pressure sensors in the seats advising the system of seat occupation. The system was inactive if the parking brake was applied.

Nineteen-seventy was the almost the last year for unbridled horsepower and there were changes to all but the base 300hp engine. A new rev-hungry solid-lifter LT1, originally destined for 1969 production and proven that year in the Camaro Z28 in 5-liter 302 form, came out a full size 350 for the Corvette, while the big-block engine choice was curtailed in range, but expanded to a monster 7.4 liters as the 454. For once, in 1970, the Corvette was trounced in the power line-up by the humble Chevelle SS454, which could be ordered with the 450hp LS6.

An aluminum-headed solid-lifter LS7 rated at 465hp was offered for 1970, but none were fitted on the St Louis assembly line. This engine was available however as a an over-the-counter crate motor, and was listed for many years in the Chevrolet Performance catalogs.

Orange valve covers indicate the base 350 cubic inch, rated 300, 270 and finally 200 horsepower over these three years. Torquey and sweet, these motors are the choice for the enthusiast who drives his Corvette often. Lack of an air cleaner decal shows this to be a 1972 200hp.

L46 350 350hp made its last appearance in 1970. This one is air-conditioned too.

By way of compensation a similarly aluminum-headed but hydraulic-lifter LS6 rated at 425hp made the otherwise de-tuned 1971 line-up.

1972 was the end of the first performance era: the LS6 was dropped and other engines nominally downrated to reflect their horsepower 'as installed', with alternators, air cleaners and full exhaust systems connected. Be in no doubt that we are now in the much longer second performance era, and to prove it just put a recent 1990 ZRI or a 2001 Z06 against the best of 1965 to 1971!

ZQ3 base 350 300hp (1970), 270hp (1971), 200hp (1972) The base 300 horsepower was still the most popular engine choice for 1970 and was an almost direct carryover from 1969. The cast iron intake manifold was now cast number 3665577 and was shared by the 350 350hp as well. It became a 3973469 for 1971 and a 6363751 for 1972, when intake runner numbers were cast in as well. The 3927186 cylinder head gave a 10.25:1 compression ratio from a 63.305cc combustion chamber.

The air cleaner was the same classic 14in open-element unit as previously until June 1970, when a chrome-topped closed dual-inlet design was adopted for the rest of this period, on all engines except LT1 and the 1971 LS6.

A reduction in compression to 8.5:1 readied this base engine for low-lead gasoline and reduced horsepower to a nominal 270hp for 1971. The pistons were now dished and the new 3973487 cylinder heads had 75.47cc combustion chambers to achieve this. The following year the same engine was re-rated with the same heads and probably the same pistons to a more honest 200hp.

The base engine had 4-bolt main bearing caps in its 300hp 1970 form and 2-bolt caps thereafter. For 1972 the left-hand exhaust manifold was no longer required to incorporate a bracket to support the alternator so a plain 2in outlet manifold (cast number 3932461) was fitted to the left-hand cylinder head.

L46 350 350hp The 1970 L46 was another carry-over from 1969 but 1970 was the last year for this classic performer. Its position as top mouse motor

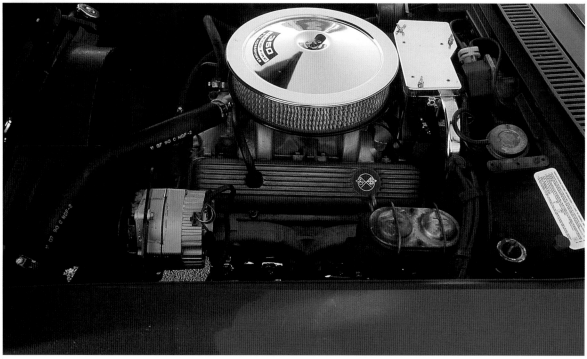

The LT1 was the top-rated small-block of the era. Redlined at 6500rpm, it was the first solid-lifter small-block since 1965, and the last to use a Holley carburetor.

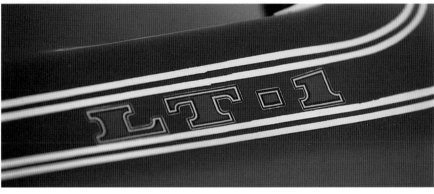

The high-rise intake manifold and Holley required the big-block hood for the style and to give clearance. Stripes were white except on light colors.

IDENTIFICATION 1970

Engine block cast numbers

350cu in	397010
454cu in	3963512

Stamped engine number suffixes

CTL	350 300hp	Rochester 4BC manual
CTD	350 300hp	Rochester 4BC manual
CTM	350 300hp	Rochester 4BC auto
CTG	350 300hp	Rochester 4BC auto
CTN	350 350hp	Rochester 4BC spec high perf, manual
CTH	350 350hp	Rochester 4BC spec high perf, manual,
CTO	350 350hp	Rochester 4BC spec high perf, manual, AC
CTJ	350 350hp	Rochester 4BC spec high perf, manual, AC
CTP	350 350hp	Rochester 4BC spec high perf, manual, TI
CTQ	350 50hp	Rochester 4BC spec high perf, manual, AC, TI
CTU	350 370hp	Holley 4BC, mech. lifters, manual, TI
CTK	350 370hp	Holley 4BC, mech. lifters, manual, TI
CTV	350 370hp	Holley 4BC, mech. lifters, manual, ZR1
CZU	454 390hp	Rochester 4BC, manual
CGW	454 390hp	Rochester 4BC, auto
CRI	454 390hp	Rochester 4BC, manual, TI
CRJ	454 390hp	Rochester 4BC, auto, TI
LQ	454 465hp	Holley 4BC, mech. lifters, alloy head, manual
LN	454 465hp	Holley 42BC, mech. lifters, alloy head, auto

Chassis numbers
194370S400001 through 194379S417316
(4th digit for a convertible is 6)

had been grabbed by the new LT1 but it still outsold the LT1 for the year by four times. It was based on a 4-bolt version of the now universal 3970010 block. The forged pistons were domed and the compression ratio 11.0:1. It was essentially now an LT1 with a Quadrajet carburetor and hydraulic lifters - in other words a troublefree LT1!

LT1 350 370hp (1970), 330hp (1971), 255hp (1972) There had been no solid-lifter small-blocks since the demise of the fuel-injected 375hp 1965 Fuel Injection, so a new rattling small-block would have been a surprise offering for 1970, had it not been already been prematurely announced for 1969. The pistons were forged with a larger dome than the L46 but the compression ratio was still rated at 11.0:1. Carburetor was a Holley on a cast 3972110 aluminum manifold, replaced by a 3959594 for 1971-72.

The new solid-lifter camshaft (part number 3972178) was similar to its 1965 predecessor but with valve lift of .458in intake and .484in exhaust, and 317°/346° duration, it had a less radical intake profile than the 1965 version. Peak torque of the LT1 was 380lb ft at 4000rpm and peak power was not developed until a warranty-threatening 6000rpm. This camshaft was used for all three years.

In 1970 25 LT1s were built as ZR1s with an M22 close-ratio 'Rockcrusher' transmission and a special brake and suspension package. A further 28 were built over the next two years.

For 1971 the compression ratio was reduced to 9.0:1 by the use of flat top pistons and output dropped to 330hp at 5600rpm, with the same camshaft. For the final year, as with the other engines, a more honest 'as installed' figure was quoted and the LT1 became a 255hp. As a compensation it was offered for this year only with air conditioning.

LS5 454 390hp (1970), 365hp (1971), 270hp (1972) If you are only ever going to own one big-block Corvette make it this one. The 1970 LS5 made 500lb ft of torque at 3400rpm. For 1972 that figure was still 390lb ft even with low-compression pistons and an honest 'as installed' SAE rating. That is still more torque than the 1993-95 multi-cam multi-valve all-aluminum LT5 developed at 4800rpm. Torque is what big-blocks are all about. Forget the aluminum-head L89 or the 425hp 396: this engine is the king. Smooth, quiet, easy-starting and with enough torque to go anywhere in top gear, this was the essence of what a big-block could be. As relaxed as a 472cu in Cadillac, this car could still blast to 60mph in 5.7 seconds. Even more impressive was the manual-transmission car's ability to climb or even accelerate up almost any hill in top gear.

In 1970 the big-block LS5 had chrome-plated pressed-steel valve covers. This was 'flash chrome', an industrial finish applied to prevent the covers rusting within the warranty period. A superb finish on these is definitely incorrect. In a return to the simplicity of 1965-67 the valve covers were once again painted in Chevrolet Orange for 1971, which made the whole engine bigger too.

The intake manifold was aluminum for 1970 only, either a 3955287 or a 3969802, and thereafter the manifolds were cast iron units from the passenger car range. The cylinder heads were cast number 3964290, almost identical to the equivalent 1969 heads except that they were now tapped for tapered spark plug seats, to match the tapered plug seat of the small-block, if not the heat range. Combustion chamber volume was 100.95cc, with valves of 2.06in inlet and 1.72in exhaust. For 1971 the 3993820 head was used with an open chamber design and a larger 113cc volume. The 1972 used a 3999241 head which was almost identical.

The 454 big-block can be used in place of the 427 block, and the cast numbers actually crossed over in Corvette applications. The 3963512 block used with a 454 crankshaft in 1970 and 1971 had been a 427 late in 1969 production, with the casting modified to allow the larger throw. The crankshaft was forged steel for strength, and unlike the 427 was externally balanced. This was achieved at the front with a counterweighted harmonic balancer, while at the drive end the manual flywheel had a cast-in counterweight and the automatic flex-plate a welded-on balance weight. For all three years 2-bolt main bearing caps retained the crankshaft in the LS5.

With typical Chevrolet good sense, the 454 connecting rod was made the same length and journal size as the 1965 396 and all the 427s. On the LS5, rod bolts were of ⅜in diameter and the piston retention was pressed pin. Pistons for 1970 were cast with a domed head, giving a compression ration of 10.25:1, while for 1971 and 1972 they were cast with a flat top and gave a compression ration of 8.5:1. Replacements today will probably be forged.

The 454 had a one-piece metal emblem and no stripes.

Opposite & Above: The LS6 was the last of the hot 454s, with just 188 made in 1971 only. Console plate tells all.

IDENTIFICATION 1971

Engine block cast numbers

350cu in	397010
454cu in	3963512

Stamped engine number suffixes

CJL	350 270hp	Rochester 4BC manual
CGT	350 270hp	Rochester 4BC auto
CJK	350 270hp	Rochester 4BC auto
CGZ	350 330hp	Holley 4BC, mech. lifters, manual
CGY	350 330hp	Holley 4BC, mech. lifters, manual, ZR1
CPH	454 365hp	Rochester 4BC manual
CPJ	454-365hp	Rochester 4BC auto
CPW	454 425hp	Holley 4BC, mech. lifters, alloy head, manual
CPX	454 425hp	Holley 4BC, mech lifters, alloy head, auto

Chassis numbers

194370S100001 through 194379S121801
(4th digit is a 6 for convertible)

OPTIONS 1970

Code	Option	Quantity	Price
19437	Base Corvette Sport Coupe	10668	$5192.00
19467	Base Corvette Convertible	6648	$4849.00
ZQ3	Base 350 300hp motor	6646	$0.00
	Base four-speed wide ratio	7806	$0.00
	Base vinyl trim	14125	$0.00
	Custom Trim leather seats	3191	$158.00
A31	Power windows	4813	$63.20
A85	Shoulder harness, std with coupe	475	$42.15
C07	Auxiliary hardtop (19467 only)	2556	$273.85
C08	Auxiliary top exterior vinyl trim	832	$63.20
C50	Rear window defroster	1281	$36.90
C60	Air conditioning	6659	$447.65
G81	Optional rear axle ratio	2862	$12.65
J50	Power brakes	8984	$47.40
L46	350 350hp engine	4910	$158.00
LS5	454 390hp engine	4473	$289.65
LT1	350 370hp engine	1287	$447.60
M21	Four-speed manual close ratio	4383	$0.00
M22	Four-speed manual heavy duty	25	$95.00
M40	Turbo Hydra-Matic transmission	5102	$0.00
Na9	California emissions equipment	1758	$36.90
N37	Tilt/telescopic steering column	5803	$84.30
N40	Power-assisted steering	11907	$105.35
P02	De Luxe wheelcovers	3467	$57.95
PT7	White stripe tires F70 x 15	6589	$31.30
PU9	White letter tires F70 x 15	7985	$33.15
T60	Heavy duty battery	165	$15.80
UA6	Alarm system	6727	$31.60
U69	AM/FM radio	14529	$172.75
U79	Stereo AM/FM radio	2462	$278.10
ZR1	Special purpose performance package	25	$968.95

The left-hand exhaust manifold was a new cast number, 3969869, while on the right-hand side the 3880828 manifold was continued as from 1966. Both would now run to the end of big-block production.

LS6 454 425hp (1971) The last gasp of the mega motors was the 1971 LS6. This was the last big-block with a Holley, the last with aluminum heads, the last with solid lifters and the last Corvette for 22 years with a quoted power output starting with a 4. Under the classic 14in open-element air filter, which it shared only with the LT1, the Holley was mounted on a 3963569 low-rise aluminum manifold. It is hard to find an aftermarket manifold to accommodate a Holley on a big-block and still close the hood, but this one does it.

The cylinder heads were aluminum with round exhaust ports, cast number 3946074 as used on the 1969 L88. Fitted with 2.19in inlet and 1.88in exhaust valves they had a combustion chamber volume of 118cc. Pistons were forged with a domed head, and gave a compression ratio of 9.0:1. I once bought a box of 80 of these brand new from an insolvent boat racer. Because they are standard bore I still have them all, but at least they are beautiful enough to sell eventually as sculpture. The solid-lifter camshaft was part number 3904362, with 0.520in intake and exhaust valve lift, first used in the 1967 427 435hp L71.

IDENTIFICATION 1972

Engine block cast numbers
350cu in	397010, 3970014
454cu in	3999289

Stamped engine number suffixes
CKW	350	200hp	Rochester 4BC manual
CDH	350	200hp	Rochester 4BC manual, NB2
CKX	350	200hp	Rochester 4BC auto
CDJ	350	200hp	Rochester 4BC auto, NB2
CKY	350	255hp	Holley 4BC, mech. lifters, manual
CRT	350	255hp	Holley 4BC, mech. lifters, manual, AIR
CKZ	350	255hp	Holley 4BC, mech. lifters, ZR1, M22 manual
CPH	454	270hp	Rochester 4BC, manual
CPJ	454	270hp	Rochester 4BC, auto
CSR	454	270hp	Rochester 4BC, manual, K19
CSS	454	270hp	Rochester 4BC, auto, K19

Chassis numbers
1Z37K2S500001 through 1Z37K2S527004
(3rd digit is a 6 for convertible, 5th digit indicates engine: K= 350 200hp, L= 350 255hp and W= 454 270hp)

1971 LS6 ZR2 If you find a 1971 LS6 you have hit gold, and if it's a ZR2 then you have struck the mother lode. Just 188 LS6s were made, plus 12 in the ZR2 specification with dual plate clutch, M22 Rock-crusher four-speed gearbox, dual-pin heavy-duty power brakes, heavy-duty suspension and aluminum radiator. Not permitted were power steering, radio or air conditioning.

In 1973 I started servicing Corvettes and Mustangs in the Tyneside area of North-east England. The second Stingray I ever worked on was a 1971 big-block four-speed belonging to a local nightclub owner. He complained of rough idle, noisy transmission, hard steering, excessive cabin heat and 'uncontrollable power'. I drove the car and was staggered by the power, which unfortunately could not be used because of a slipping clutch which still had an amazingly light pedal. A few days later the car was in my backyard shop for a tune-up, brake pads and a new 11in clutch which I had specially ordered in. I was disappointed to find the new brake pads would not fit, I could not remove the plugs which were frozen into the aluminum heads, and when I came to fit the clutch I found that it was a strange little dual-plate device. Well it didn't need plugs and the dual pin pads were only half worn, but the clutch took months to get. With the float level and timing adjusted and the clutch finally installed I took it for the essential test drive – and returned the car grinning and glowing with the experience. The owner still hated it and next day the car was taken to London and traded against a 1972 Mach I Mustang. I never saw it again. Only when I first saw Karl Ludvigsens's book *Corvette - America's Star Spangled Sports Car* did I realize that this car was one of only 12 ZR2s. I then discovered that it had been shipped to Europe to compete in Italy's Targa Florio – and failed to get an entry. I searched hard

454 cars with air conditioning used this unique long brass coolant expansion tank.

Corvette radios have always been factory fitted, and paid for as options. More than one million radios at an average cost of $200 per unit – and most other sports car makers didn't even provide the aperture to fit one. AM/FM selector also flipped the face, and stereo units had indicator lamp at top right of the face, or dial as we called it then.

There were no Corvette power antennas for ten years from 1967. The ball-ended tapered stainless antenna was simpler and prettier, and could be quickly removed and stowed if required.

Mid-1971 wiper motor had an integral pump for pulsed washers. Earlier models had five pipes here, the two extra being for the headlight washers.

OPTIONS 1971

Code	Option	Quantity	Price
19437	Base Corvette Sport Coupe	14680	$5496.00
19467	Base Corvette Convertible	7121	$5259.00
ZQ3	Base 350 270hp motor	14547	$0.00
	Base four-speed wide ratio	9224	$0.00
	Base vinyl trim	19199	$0.00
	Custom Trim leather seats	2602	$158.00
A31	Power windows	6192	$79.00
A85	Shoulder harness, std with coupe	677	$42.00
C07	Auxiliary hardtop (19467 only)	2619	$274.00
C08	Auxiliary top exterior vinyl trim	832	$63.00
C50	Rear window defroster	1598	$42.00
C60	Air conditioning	11481	$459.00
J50	Power brakes	13558	$47.00
LS5	454 365hp engine	5097	$295.00
LS6	454 425hp engine	188	$1221.00
LT1	350 330hp engine	1949	$483.00
M21	Four-speed manual close ratio	2387	$0.00
M22	Four-speed manual heavy duty	130	$100.00
M40	Turbo Hydra-Matic transmission	10060	$0.00
N37	Tilt/telescopic steering column	8130	$84.30
N40	Power-assisted steering	17904	$115.90
P02	De Luxe wheelcovers	3007	$63.00
PT7	White stripe tires F70 x 15	6711	$28.00
PU9	White letter tires F70 x 15	12449	$42.00
T60	Heavy duty battery	1455	$15.80
U69	AM/FM radio	21509	$178.00
U79	Stereo AM/FM radio	3431	$283.00
ZR1	330hp Special purpose perf. package	8	$1010.00
ZR2	425hp Special purpose perf. package	12	1747.00

As always since 1961, the twin rear lamps were contrived to reflect in the rear bumpers. Mid-1971 and later lenses had rounded centers like these.

Outer headlamp washers were discontinued in early 1971.

for it and was told it had been exported to the Gulf States, but then it turned up in the north of England a few years back, and so now I have the frustrating pleasure of signing the insurance valuation for the new owner every year.

1970 & 1971 LT1 ZRI The ZR1 was produced as a special-purpose off-road car with the LT1 small-block and essentially the same options and restrictions as the ZR2. Like its big brother it would be very hard to be certain of its pedigree without seeing the original gas tank sticker, and many second and later owners probably never knew what they had. It is believed that 25 were made in 1970 and another eight in 1971.

COOLING SYSTEM

At first glance 1970-72 Corvettes would appear to have been sent out with a bewildering variety of copper or aluminum radiators, plastic or metal shrouds and aluminum, brass or no coolant expansion tanks. But just as in 1969, there was a cool logic behind all the cooling choices, determined by simple rules.

The Harrison aluminum radiator used a stamped steel shroud except on ZRs, had no provision for an automatic-transmission cooler, or a radiator cap, and always used the 5in diameter aluminum expansion tank with neck and 15lb cap. The copper radiator was used for all automatics, air-conditioned cars and LT1s except ZRs. It had a plastic shroud and was direct filled. Additionally, all air-conditioned big-blocks used a 20in long soldered brass expansion tank with a filler and 15lb cap. By this stage cooling was not a problem, even on air-conditioned big-blocks.

EMISSIONS SYSTEM

Not all 1970-1972 cars were equipped with AIR, as they had been in 1969. Except for cars destined for California, the following were not equipped with AIR and therefore were a joy to behold with the hood open: 1971 350 300, 350 350 and 454 LS5, 1972 350 270 and 454 LS5, and 1972 350 200.

ELECTRICS

In mid-1971 the innovative headlamp washers were discontinued. The front parking lenses were changed from clear to amber in the early part of the same year. The previously optional anti-theft alarm was made standard for 1972.

The alternator was now mounted on its own bracket directly to the newly provided holes on the front of the cylinder head, rather than to the exhaust manifold as previously.

All batteries were of the side terminal type. In 1972 lighter and cheaper copper-clad aluminum

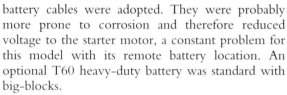

P02 wheel covers would last on the option list until 1973, while the Rally wheel combination remained the base for the whole C3 era. Sensibly, both these owners run radial tires.

battery cables were adopted. They were probably more prone to corrosion and therefore reduced voltage to the starter motor, a constant problem for this model with its remote battery location. An optional T60 heavy-duty battery was standard with big-blocks.

TRANSMISSIONS

During this period there was a gradual move towards 11.0in rather than the 10.4in single-disc clutches. Often the 10.4in was found with the higher-performance engines. It is generally essential to remove the clutch to find the size before ordering a replacement. The superb but expensive 10.0in dual-plate clutch used with the ZR2 and sometimes optional was discontinued after 1971, as was the M22 'Rock Crusher' Muncie four-speed.

1971 saw the introduction of fine-splined input and output shafts on the Muncie. While there was presumably an engineering advantage to this, in practical terms it made it much easier to refit the gearbox after a clutch change, and earned Chevrolet the gratitude of mechanics and hobbyists everywhere.

WHEELS & TIRES

Rally wheels and trims or optional full wheelcovers continued as from 1969. Blackwall F70 x 15 bias-ply nylon tires were supplied by Goodyear or Firestone as base equipment. The optional white stripe tires were Goodyear Speedway Wide Tread and Firestone Super Sport Wide Oval. The Firestones had a slightly wider tread and were the contemporary enthusiast's choice. Raised white letter tires were Goodyear Wide Tread or Firestone Wide O Oval. It is possible that there were some Uniroyal Tiger Paws white letter tires fitted in 1972 only. It would be foolhardy to run any of the above

at significant speed on today's roads when the full performance of these cars can be safely enjoyed on modern radial tires.

SUSPENSION & BRAKES

After six years of the F41 optional suspension the option was dropped for 1970-72, and just as it was part of the 1963 Z06 package, special suspension and brakes were fitted only to ZR1 and ZR2 cars.

	OPTIONS 1972		
Code	Option	Quantity	Price
19437	Base Corvette Sport Coupe	20496	$5533.00
19467	Base Corvette Convertible	6508	$5296.00
ZQ3	Base 350 200hp motor	14547	$0.00
	Base four-speed wide ratio	10803	$0.00
	Base vinyl trim	18295	$0.00
	Custom Trim leather seats	8709	$158.00
A31	Power windows	9495	$83.35
A85	Shoulder harness, std with coupe	749	$42.15
C07	Auxiliary hardtop (19467 only)	2646	$273.85
C08	Auxiliary top exterior vinyl trim	811	$158.00
C50	Rear window defroster	2221	$42.15
C60	Air conditioning	17011	$464.50
J50	Power brakes	18770	$47.40
K19	Air injection reactor	1912	$0.00
LS5	454 270hp engine	3913	$294.90
LT1	350 255hp engine	1741	$483.45
M21	Four-speed manual close ratio	1638	$0.00
M40	Turbo Hydra-Matic transmission	14543	$0.00
NB2	California emissions equipment	1766	$0.00
N37	Tilt/telescopic steering column	12992	$84.30
N40	Power-assisted steering	23794	$115.90
P02	De Luxe wheelcovers	3593	$63.20
PT7	White stripe tires F70 x 15	6666	$30.35
PU9	White letter tires F70 x 15	16623	$43.65
T60	Heavy duty battery	2969	$15.80
U69	AM/FM radio	19480	$178.00
U79	Stereo AM/FM radio	7189	$283.35
ZR1	330hp Special purpose perf. package	20	$1,010.05

1973

At the time of writing, the Corvette is approaching its half century. Soon it will have been around for more than half the total time that cars have been made and driven. This is an extraordinary achievement, and proof that the formula of a large-engined, American-built fiberglass-bodied two-seater is one that works.

The Corvette has also succeeded because the engineers and stylists have adapted the car when necessary to accommodate changes in taste, driving habits, lifestyle and, particularly in the 1970s, changes in the law. Chevrolet has never shied away from spending money, not only to update the car to meet legal requirements but also to actually improve it at the same time. Just how well they could achieve this was shown with the September 1972 launch of the 1973 Corvette. Faced with dual challenge of cleaning up the emissions of two different V8 engines and redesigning for an onerous 2.5mph barrier test, it would have been easy for Chevrolet to consign the Corvette to the history

books after 20 good years. We should be grateful that they didn't.

BODY & BODY TRIM

The 2.5mph barrier test required the car to be driven into a solid concrete wall and reverse away with all lighting and control systems intact. Happily, Chevrolet determined that the best way to do this was with a complex bumper system disguised behind a deformable polyurethane body-colored cover, which they called a fascia.

Perhaps the greatest virtue of the shark body design is its long nose. Long enough to house a straight-12, it actually enclosed a choice of two big but compact V8s. While other European manufacturers tacked heavy-looking separate rubber bumpers onto their US export lines, Chevrolet made a virtue of necessity: to meet the new regulations for 1973 the company extended the long-nose design and made it even longer and more attractive.

Longer nose for 1973 suited the Stingray shape as well as modernizing it.

DIMENSIONS & WEIGHTS	
Length	184.7in
Width	69.2in
Height	
Sport Coupe	47.75in
Convertible	47.8in
Wheelbase	98.0in
Max track	
Front	58.7in
Rear	59.4in
Curb weight	
Sport Coupe	3407lb
Convertible	3414lb

Polyurethane nose concealed a steel bumper mechanism that met new Federal crash regulations. Tail was unchanged from 1972. This convertible has light modifications for UK use.

Opposite top: Coupe rear window was now fixed. The rack was a dealer-supplied addition. Opposite bottom: British-owned 454 LS4 with correct deep rubber air deflector to improve engine cooling on air-conditioned big-blocks.

Certainly the 1973 model indicated the beginning of a radical change of direction for the Corvette. Press comment at the time was mainly negative, but when I saw the October 1972 *Corvette News* announcing the new 1973 I was immediately impressed. Having owned my 1966 for three years by this time, here I felt was a car which could aspire to replace my Sting Ray. Much of the story related to the standard fitment of radial tires, which I had been running for years, and it seemed that at last Chevrolet was directing its sports car towards the future. It had great-looking optional eight-slot alloy wheels, the first time that an optional alloy wheel had been offered since 1967 - although we did not know then that these wheels would be postponed until 1976. The new body looked much more streamlined, which would make it quieter inside and better suited to long fast journeys than my noisy and leaky 327 350 1966 convertible. Considerable sales capital was made out of the new cushioned body-mount system, better sound proofing and larger-capacity mufflers. Evidently others felt the same, for the '73 would go on to be the best-selling Corvette over a normal-length production year so far.

The new soft nose assembly actually extended the overall length of the car by just 2.2 inches. Visually, however, it was much longer than the chrome-bumpered nose it replaced. Manufactured of a flexible urethane, it would deform in an impact and then revert to its original shape, hopefully shedding not too much of its flexibly formulated paint. Unfortunately heat and perhaps ultra-violet light degraded the urethane plastic material, allowing it to go brittle and then crumble, in southern states at least. Today's replacements have taken advantage of advances in plastics technology and are much superior.

Like the 1968-72 models previously described, the 1973 had paired intake grilles between the front bumperettes and the parking lamps, as well as a central grille. In terms of the intake of cooling air these were probably secondary to the main intake, which was below the car in front of the main radiator. These grilles were cast aluminum alloy, finished in matt black and incorporating the mounting for the parking lamps. Uniquely on the 1973, the leading edge of the grille slats and matching ribs on the clear plastic lamp assembly were accented with silver paint. The optional front license plate bracket could either be fitted in front of the center grille, or replace it to recess the plate between the overriders.

Between the headlight lids a new emblem was introduced, a cloisonné red sunburst behind the traditional Corvette crossed flags, ringed with the words 'Chevrolet Motor Division Corvette', while the previous years' crossed flags emblem still remained on the gas filler lid.

The complex concealed windshield wiper system was abandoned, the wipers now lifting out of a

COLORS

Code	Body	Suggested interior trim
910	Classic white	Black, Dark Red, Dark Saddle, Midnight Blue, Medium Saddle
914	Silver	Black, Dark Red, Dark Saddle, Midnight Blue, Medium Saddle
922	Medium Blue	Black, Midnight Blue, Medium Saddle
927	Dark Blue	Black, Dark Red, Midnight Blue, Medium Saddle
945	Blue Green	Black, Dark Red, Dark Saddle, Medium Saddle
947	Elkhart Green	Black, Medium Saddle
952	Yellow	Black, Dark Saddle, Midnight Blue
953	Metallic Yellow	Black, Midnight Blue
976-	Mille Miglia Red	Black, Dark Red, Dark Saddle, Midnight Blue, Medium Saddle
980	Orange	Black, Medium Saddle

All wheels were Argent Silver. Convertible top choice was Black or White. Custom leather interior was Black, Medium Saddle and Dark Saddle only.

trough behind the flipped-up edge of the hood. This treatment had been extended to most GM cars at the time, the big sedans in 1968 and the Camaro and Firebird in 1970. Air flow to the interior heating and cooling system was certainly improved as a consequence of removing the flap and grille.

The hood panel was all new. Now the same for both 350 and 454 engined cars, it featured a body-colored metal grille at the rear of the raised center panel. This grille was the intake for a cold air induction system. Originally developed by GM engineer Vince Piggins, this device was first seen on 1969 production-line cars fitted to the Corvette L-88 described above and on the Camaro Z28. As then, the idea was to duct cold and therefore dense outside air from the pressurized zone at the base of the windshield directly to the air cleaner and carburetor, thus improving the density of the engine's intake air. All Corvettes since then have used variations on this system, though since 1976 the air has generally been sourced from the high-pressure area ahead of the radiator.

In the 1973 system, which would continue unchanged through 1975, the cold intake remained closed until a throttle switch flipped open a solenoid-actuated door just beneath the grille. Under hard acceleration, a wonderful moaning roar is heard from this device, more V12 than V8, which never fails to impress. Switching occurs at two-thirds throttle opening. To subdue underhood noise and meet new Federal noise regulations, a soft fiberglass sound-absorbing pad was fixed to the hood panel with large round retainers on bonded pins. To the consternation of many concours d'elegance entrants since, this could burst into flames when soaked with a few years of engine oil and subjected to reflected sunshine from an incorrect chrome-plated air filter lid.

To accommodate the new nose, and to allow for the new open wiper trough, the front upper surround panel was revised from the 1972 version. The lower fenders were also revised, at the front to meet the new soft nose and behind the wheel with the new simplified and streamlined engine air outlet.

CHASSIS

By 1973 the frame was into its second decade of production, already old fashioned in concept but earning General Motors handsome profits as sales increased. The cult status of the Corvette ensured that however much journalists criticized it, the car went on selling despite its weight, thirst and body flex. In a world of continuous change and improvement there is plenty of appeal in a constant and unchanging design, and the Corporation was happy to oblige.

The big change for the year was the new flexible bodymount system. Apparently mindful of the

Simplified fender outlets (left) matched the plain new nose. Expensive cloisonné nose emblem (below) was a curious choice for a sports car but now has a period feel.

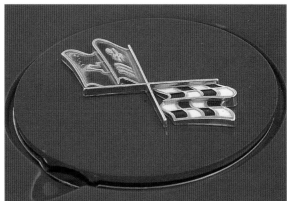

The 1973 gas filler lid emblem remained the same from 1968 to 1982.

The door handles always mystified newcomers but worked well.

The stylish but sometimes troublesome wiper flap was replaced by a new full-length hood (above) with a larger bulge to fit both 350 and 454 motors, and a working cold air intake system. Grilles were cast alloy (right), painted black with bright front edges. The cold air hood (far right) drew pressurized air from the base of the windshield. Its intake flap was throttle pedal controlled.

effects that fitting radial tires would have on ride, perceived vibration and harshness, the engineers intriduced new bodymount donuts to replace the previous thin rubber mounts. The body was thus raised an inch, giving useful scope for larger tires in the future. It is not certain whether the practise of shimming the body to compensate for variations in the frame ceased at this time. It would require a gross error to need compensation above that offered by the flexible mounts. The flexible mounts can be retrofitted to earlier cars using the same frame to

Not visible but easily appreciated were the new cushioned body mounts, which also raised the body on the chassis.

achieve a better ride, though this practise is less popular than it was. Care must be taken in mounting the bumpers on earlier cars too if this modification is adopted. There is another possible reason for the thicker bodymount introduced for 1973. Raising the body by an inch may just have helped correct the bumper height to the Federally required level, though this was never mentioned at the time.

The frame was more or less a repeat of the 1972 pattern apart from the new bolt holes required at the front for the new absorption system. This was an ingenious and simple solution to Federal requirements, and interestingly went no further than was required by the law. In the event of a front impact, the inner metal bumper bar and its support assembly were free to move backward by up to 3½ inches in slots provided in the frame extension. This movement was limited by two energy-absorbing bolts which were reduced in diameter by being drawn through a pair of die nuts, a process similar to the manufacture by extrusion of steel wire. Following a front-end impact, according to Chevrolet it was only necessary to change the inner bumper and the drawbolts; the nose urethane would recover its shape.

Of course these were theoretical impacts, and the barrier had to be at 90 degrees to the direction of travel – move that wheel a touch, make that angle 70 degrees, and the nose and impact assembly are all pushed sideways and ruined! The frame usually needs straightening too. Having repaired quite a few '73 and '74 Corvettes with front end damage and parted out more that were wrecked, I have only ever seen one drawbolt that was even slightly extruded.

Standard door trim (left) with no power window. Convertible doors had a pin and socket at the rear to help prevent shake. Visors (below) were Comfort-weave even if seats were leather.

So is this a criticism of the GM engineers? Absolutely not! They designed a lightweight and ingenious device that exactly satisfied the specified demand of the Federal law - and no more. The rival MGB and Jaguar XJS arrived off the boats with black rubber battering rams on their previously elegant fronts, while Chevrolet made their car more elegant. Again and again the history of the Corvette demonstrates the virtue of spending time on the drawing board, researching, testing and simply spending the money to develop and perfect a design. The British engineers looked at the new US bumper regulations and decided that if the Yanks wanted battering rams then that was what they would jolly well get. The Corvette by contrast represents the triumph of design over expediency.

INTERIOR

On entering the new 1973 Corvette, the experienced owner of a previous model would immediately notice the heavier doors which were the consequence of the new federally required side-entry barriers. Beneath, the bright metal trims on the pedal rubbers, the rotating knob and vacuum over-ride switch were all now gone.

The rear view mirror was unique to 1973, eight inches long and black plastic backed, unless the new-for-1973 UF1 map light mirror was ordered. This mirror had a map reading lens with a slider switch operating only when the ignition was on. There were few other interior changes from 1972. Optional de luxe leather interior colors had been cut back to just Saddle and Black in 1970. Now an additional Dark Saddle was offered, while in keeping with the more somber colors of the period, Dark Red replaced Red and was offered in vinyl only.

The other change was prompted by the omission of the removable rear window. The drop-down storage shelf for this was no longer needed, increasing luggage space and removing a persistent source of rattles. The forced air C50 optional rear window defogger remained: while it would have been simpler to use a heated-wire defogger on the now permanently bonded back window in the coupe, the C50 was still needed for the convertible and detachable hardtop.

Comfort-weave fabric was never as nice as leather, and as seats aged they would appear to be covered in beach sand – actually the dried-out foam leaching through the open-weave fabric. Map pocket (right) had concealed springs to keep its shape.

INSTRUMENTS & CONTROLS

Instrument color was now white letters on black, as introduced in 1972. This would be the last year in which it was possible to have a major oil leak in the cabin due to the failure of the flexible plastic pipe connecting the mechanical oil pressure gauge to the engine. Experience shows, however, that an obvious break behind the firewall is preferable to an

Black leather coupe interior. Stitching pattern was across the car for leather. Center cushion is an essential accessory for long drives and protects the frail parking brake console too.

By 1973 the vast majority of Corvettes were fitted with power steering but only about half had the tilt/telescopic steering column. Both are worth fitting.

undetected break on the engine side because the oil pan will empty in less than a half a minute at speed.

ENGINES

L48 350 190hp For 1973 the base engine, now known as L48, was rated 10 horsepower down on the 1972 at a meagre 190hp. This was the first time since the 1955 introduction of the V8 as a 265cu in engine that a Corvette was offered with such low quoted power. In reality, of course, the old gross horsepower system of 1955 would have tested the 1973 engine at about 225hp, but it was still a depressing situation for the performance-hungry.

This was an engine that was still running a dual exhaust and no catalytic converters, but General Motors had a new mission - to meet seemingly impossible emissions and fuel economy targets that were destined to become even more onerous towards the end of the century. Low compression ratios, gentle camshafts and retarded ignition timing were then the only solutions available to achieve these figures. Billions of research dollars would be spent by General Motors, Ford and Chrysler over the next two decades, and GM fans can be proud that it was that Corporation that did most to keep the V8 dream alive.

Owners of this engine today should remember that there is no easier or cheaper V8 than the small-block to rebuild and modify. Without affecting the external appearance of the engine at all, higher compression pistons, larger valves, more aggressive

The base 350 shown was now rated at 190 hp, while the optional new L82 gave 250hp, very close to the now dropped LT1 and without the trouble of solid lifters. Auto shift lever (below) controlled almost indestructible Turbo Hydra-Matic 400.

camshafts and gas-flowed combustion chambers can improve performance way beyond anything that was lost back in the early '70s.

Starting from the top, the L48 used a 7043202 Rochester four-barrel Quadrajet with the base four-speed manual transmission, or 7043203 with the optional automatic transmission. The choke was thermostatic, with a heat coil on the intake manifold. The air cleaner was an entirely new design that worked in conjunction with the new cold air induction system. It consisted of a round rubber seal which fitted onto a flange, which in turn clipped into the outer air cleaner bowl. Within this was the AC A329C filter element, topped with a plain gloss black lid. The recommended filter was later changed to an A348C, which became the standard in 1974 and gave more filtration area.

The intake manifold was cast iron 3997770, or 3997771, with for the first time an EGR (exhaust gas recirculation) valve. This device diluted the incoming mixture charge with exhaust gas sourced from the crossover passage in the manifold, and reduced combustion temperature and therefore emissions of nitrous oxides. It was vacuum operated to function only at wider throttle openings. When failed in the open position it will prevent the car running at low engine speed. The EGR is easily and often disabled. The intake manifold was painted engine orange and was also used by the 250hp L82.

Cylinder heads were as for 1972, cast number 3998993, and had 1.94in inlet and 1.50in exhaust valves. It is possible that heads cast 333881 and 333882 were also used. All had hardened valve seats to suit unleaded gasoline. Valve covers were plain stamped steel, painted orange.

The cylinder block for both the 1973 small-block Corvettes was the ubiquitous 3970010, used for the whole 1970s decade. A very few early production '73s had a cast 3970014 cylinder block, cast at Tonowanda but machined at Flint. Therefore they had the cast date in the Tonowanda big-block style showing the year as two figures, 73, rather than the single figure 3 as used by Flint. The crankshaft was nodular iron and in the 190hp L48 it ran 2-bolt main bearing caps. Pistons were cast aluminum, dished for valve clearance, giving a compression ratio of 8.5:1. Camshaft design was unchanged from the base 300hp engine of 1970.

The distributor was the familiar Delco Remy with tachometer drive, numbered 1112098 on the wrap band.

All 1973 Corvettes came fitted with air-injection reactor systems, and almost all have since been removed! This was the first time since 1968 that an entire year's production was thus equipped. The systems are complex, spoil the underhood appearance and add nothing to the performance or economy of the car. Their contribution to overall emissions is slight because their main use is to reduce them during start and warm-up. NCRS judging quite rightly requires the AIR system to be in place on cars thus originally equipped, because this is the way they left the factory. Whatever one's own feelings there may be some who thrill to the flat beating sound of a properly installed pump or who can tell a correctly working diverter valve even during a full throttle shift – and most importantly there must be an EPA official somewhere who is even now restoring a Stingray...

On all 1973s, the pump is aluminum, with the number 7801149 on its cast iron backplate. The pulley on both small-block motors is stamped 3917234. As on earlier mouse motors, the bracket is cast 3923214. The diverter valve is stamped 7029199 and the check valves are stamped 5361992.

Exhaust manifolds are cast 3932461, this being the cast iron ram's horn 2in-outlet unit first used on the 1970 LT1, drilled and tapped to take the AIR fittings. The exhaust system was fully dual and of 2in diameter carbon steel. For 1973 new larger and quieter mufflers were introduced which differed from previous years in having a chrome plated tip with a central inlet. The mufflers were made in one piece with the intermediate exhaust pipes. Reproductions are now available and generally give a superb fit.

L82 350 250hp The new optional high-performance small-block engine for 1973 was the L82. This was considered a special treat for Corvette owners because no other model apart from the Z28 Camaro was offered with an optional small-block engine. Hailed as a replacement for the 1970-72 LT1, it lacked that legendary unit's solid lifters and cam, Holley carburetor and aluminum intake manifold. Rated at a lower 250hp than the 255 of the last 1972 LT1, it at least managed an

IDENTIFICATION

Engine block cast numbers

350cu in	3970010
454cu in	3999289

Stamped engine number suffixes

CKZ	350 190hp	Rochester 4BC manual
CLA	350 190hp	Rochester 4BC auto
CLB	350 190hp	Rochester 4BC manual, Calif
CLC	350 190hp	Rochester 4BC auto, Calif
CLD	350 250hp	Rochester 4BC auto
CLH	350 250hp	Rochester 4BC auto, Calif
CLR	350 250hp	Rochester 4BC manual
CLS	350 250hp	Rochester 4BC manual, Calif
CWM	454 275hp	Rochester 4BC manual
CWR	454 275hp	Rochester 4BC auto
CWS	454 275hp	Rochester 4BC auto, Calif
CWT	454 275hp	Rochester 4BC manual, Calif

Chassis numbers

1Z37J3S400001 through 1Z37J3S434464
(3rd digit is a 6 for convertible. 5th digit indicates engine: J=350 190hp, T=350 250hp and Z=454 275hp)

Big-block LS4 used same cold air system as small-blocks. All Corvettes would now have cold air induction.

extra 5lb ft of torque, giving 285lb ft at 4000rpm. The L48 was managing 275lb ft at a lowly 2800rpm, emphasizing the problems of trying to make a high-performance optional engine in this climate. But this engine cannot be dismissed, for it would go on to wave the flag for Corvette through the lean years of fuel crises and emission-led downsizing, and with almost 60,000 units supplied over eight years it is the most popular Corvette optional engine ever.

This must have taken some determined arguing by those brave suited champions of the Corvette in the endless General Motors committee meetings. 'Why should we gamble on V8s at all?', they must have wondered as they watched the once-mighty Mustang morph into a six-cylinder shopping car, or Chrysler, guardians of the Hemi heritage and the incredible 300 series cars, reduced to building poor copies of rivals' models on an undersized front wheel drive four-cylinder platform and apparently making money at the same time.

The progress of the L82 is worth watching over this next eight years, and it is also worth comparing it to the extraordinary progress closer to our own time of the stock Corvette engine from 1984 to 1992, when horsepower leapt from 205 to 300hp and fuel economy improved by more than 30 per cent too.

The L82 used a 7043212 Quadrajet on the automatic cars or a 7043213 on the base four-speeds. Intake manifold was cast iron 3997771, similar to the base engine's, and painted orange.

Cylinder heads were cast 330545, with valve head diameters of 2.02in inlet and 1.60in exhaust, and were topped with the same finned alloy valve covers first seen on the 1969 optional small-block engines. This head had screw-in rocker studs and pushrod guide plates in anticipation of the heavy-duty use expected of an optional engine. As in the superseded LT1, pistons were forged rather than cast, flat-topped with a valve relief notch, and gave a compression ratio of 9.0:1.

The connecting rods were forged steel, shot peened, heat treated and magnafluxed with rod bolts. The 3970010 block was machined for 4-bolt main bearing caps, which restrained a forged crankshaft. The high-lift camshaft, cast 3896964, gave intake and exhaust lift of .450in and .460in respectively. A new camshaft perhaps for 1973? No, this was the high-performance hydraulic cam last seen on the 1969-70 L46 350 350, and prior to that on the 1965-68 L79 327 350. The distributor was numbered 1112150.

Exhaust manifolds were the same as the L-48's, but a 2.5in dual exhaust system was fitted, the front pipes having 2in adapters welded into the 2.5in just below each exhaust manifold.

Only a passing knowledge of V8 engines is needed to see that here was a super-strong engine fading away for want of some proper compression. This was easily achieved in different ways, and whether it was legal depended on the particular state's inspection policy. The cheapest solution - but requiring engine removal - was to fit at least 10:1 compression pistons. Leaving the engine in place it was easy to fit smaller-chamber heads. Today we have excellent aluminum heads available, which because of their better conductivity will even allow running unleaded gasoline without excessive detonation. Or for the brave this engine was more than strong enough to take some real boost from a compact underhood supercharger...

LS4 454 275hp The LS4 big-block 454 replaced the 1972 LS5, and gained a nominal 5 horsepower to be rated at 275hp. Knowledgeable V8 enthusiasts compare torque figures and not horsepower - indeed horsepower was omitted from the console data plates from 1972 onwards - and by this measure the 454 is by far the most powerful engine. It produced 380lb ft at a gentle 2800rpm against the L82's 280lb ft at a raucous 4000rpm.

Looking at this engine in detail, it varied from the 1972 454 in a number of ways. The carburetor was a Quadrajet 7043200 with the TH400 automatic, or a 7043201 with the four-speed, mounted on a new-for-1973 low-rise cast iron intake manifold cast 353015. This was similar to the previous manifold but for the addition of an EGR valve toward the left front of the manifold, opposite the position used on small-block manifolds.

Cylinder heads were cast 353049, essentially similar to the 1972 454 head with oval ports, 2.06in inlet and 1.72in exhaust valves and a 113.06cc chamber volume. The lower half of the 1973 454 engine was the same as the 1972, with the same 3999289 block, but as discussed above the camshaft was different. It was cast number 353041, with lift of .440in inlet and .440in exhaust, and duration of 346° and 348° respectively. The distributor was labelled 1112114 and plug wires were the usual metal braid-covered big-block type, unless the radio was not ordered.

Exhaust manifolds and pipes were as before, except that the new 1973-only rectangular tip outlets with central inlet pipe were used, behind 2.5in mufflers and intermediate pipes that were shared with the L82. All 1973 454s were redlined at 5600rpm, a figure which this author firmly advises his friends and customers never to even contemplate. Peak torque of the LS4 is at 2800rpm: use it!

At $250 the LS4 was a cheaper option than the $295 L82, and it included a rear sway bar and linkage assembly not otherwise available on the small-block cars unless option ZO7 was chosen. Additionally, big-block owners got the new one-piece 454 emblem on either side of the hood, while L82 customers got nothing at all.

The futuristic wiper flap was gone, and the hood was now longer instead.

Headlights were unchanged, but parking and side marker lamps were both new designs.

Radio knobs now used a semi-quaver and a radiating transmitter to indicate volume and tuning functions.

COOLING SYSTEM

All 1973 Corvettes benefited from a new coolant recovery system and a new larger radiator core. Aluminum radiators were now discontinued. A translucent plastic bottle was located in the space behind the right-hand inner fender connected by a rubber tube. A 15lb RC33 radiator cap was fitted to the right-hand end of the radiator and excess coolant expanded into the recovery bottle, to be drawn back by vacuum as the engine cooled. The advantage of this system was that it allowed the owner to top up his coolant to a visible level without the risk of opening a pressurized cap. Previous Corvette systems often looked similar but on these the remote bottle was always pressurized. Addicts of Corvette ephemera will recall the exception to be the aluminum high-performance radiators of 1959-60 which incorporated an unpressurized reservoir.

Both radiator and shroud were rationalized for 1973 by using the same units for both big- and small block-motors. A choice of two shroud extensions accommodated the different length motors. To assist air to enter the radiator, a black plastic air deflector was fixed behind the three-holed lower valance panel. Chevrolet recommended their dealers to add a rubber extension to this deflector on air-conditioned LS4s.

ELECTRICS

The Guide T-3 sealed beam headlamps, which were a feature for so long, were replaced in 1973 by Guide Power Beams. The headlamp bezel material changed to fiberglass in early 1973 production. Since 1968 they had been diecast aluminum. The side marker lamps were a new design, manufactured in diecast aluminum with an amber lens, which was bonded into place and not replaceable. The rear side marker lenses, and rear lamps, were as previously used on the 1970-72.

In an attempt to make more occupants wear seat belts, 1973 cars had pressure sensors in the seat cushions, and a seat belt warning light and buzzer. To extinguish the alarm buzzer when the seat was occupied, the seat belt had to be extended. The buzzer did not sound if an automatic car was in reverse, or if the parking brake was applied. Inevitably, it is quite rare to find these systems in full working order today, but the parts are available to those who care.

TRANSMISSIONS

The trend towards more automatics continued with 58 per cent opting for the Turbo Hydra-Matic 400, an exact carryover from the previous year. The standard transmission was still the wide-ratio

These YJ8 eight-slot aluminum wheels were fitted to a few hundred early 1973s before they were withdrawn. That makes them at least acceptable on any 1973, a model they suit particularly well.

Muncie, the maincase cast 3925661 exactly as per 1972. The close-ratio 'box was in the same case, also a carryover, and chosen by twice as many as in 1972. Date code suffix letters were also the same. The M22 was discontinued and not offered on any other Chevrolet model either.

WHEELS & TIRES

All the launch pictures for the 1973 coupe showed it wearing the new optional YJ8 eight-slot cast aluminum wheels. They were exactly right for the Corvette, modernized it just when it was needed, and saved a useful 8lb of unsprung weight over each Rally wheel, particularly as the spare was also aluminum.

Incredibly, although 800 sets were manufactured it is believed that only 4 sets were actually fitted at the St Louis assembly plant. It is said that porosity was the problem, leading to deflation of the tubeless tires. For whatever reason, the wheels were not finally released until the 1976 model year. An original 1973 set would carry the casting number 329381 and the broadcast code letters XM. A date code would also be evident, 'mmddyy', with the 'yy' being '72 or '73. The exposed lug nuts were unique to this year because the top of the nut was painted black. 1973 owners have no shame about running the identical 1976-79 eight-slot wheels on their cars - the car was styled to wear them and they look great.

De luxe PO2 wheelcovers were offered for the last time this year. While sales of these radial-finned covers had exceeded 3000 per year since 1970, only 1739 were sold in 1973, perhaps because stock was now depleted.

The Rally wheel carried on as the stock wheel, so 1973 becomes the only year until 1982 in which there were, if only briefly, three different wheel appearance choices.

Radial tires at last appeared on the Corvette in 1973. Enthusiasts had been fitting them to their Corvettes for years, and they were obviously so superior that it was hard to believe that the car's manufacturer had not noticed their many advantages. Firestone and Goodyear were not exactly in the forefront of radial tire design at this time and, as we have already seen, the pace of technical progress during the 1970s was very slow.

Chevrolet finally went for radial tires in 1973, but owners had already been fitting them for years previously and enjoying the benefits of much improved ride, grip and road feel. These 1978 wheels (below) are very close to the withdrawn 1973 eight-slots. Most 1973s were supplied with the base Rally wheel (opposite), a Chevrolet design icon.

OPTIONS

Code	Option	Quantity	Price
1YZ37	Base Corvette Sport Coupe	25521	$5561.00
1YZ67	Base Corvette Convertible	4943	$5398.00
L48	Base 350 190hp motor	20342	$0.00
	Base four-speed wide ratio	8833	$0.00
	Base vinyl trim	17030	$0.00
	Custom Trim leather seats	13434	$154.00
A31	Power windows	14024	$83.00
A85	Shoulder harness, std with coupe	788	$41.00
C07	Auxiliary Hardtop (YZ67 only)	1328	$267.00
C08	Auxiliary top exterior vinyl trim	323	$62.00
C50	Rear window defroster	4412	$41.00
C60	Air conditioning	21578	$452.00
J50	Power brakes	24168	$46.00
LS4	454 275hp engine	4412	$250.00
L82	350 250hp engine	5710	$299.00
M21	Four-speed manual close ratio	3704	$0.00
M40	Turbo Hydra-Matic transmission	17927	$0.00
N37	Tilt/telescopic steering column	17949	$82.00
N40	Power-assisted steering	27872	$113.00
P02	De luxe wheelcovers	1739	$62.00
QRM	White stripe radials GR70 x 15	19903	$32.00
QRZ	White letter radials GR70 x 15	4541	$45.00
T60	Heavy duty battery	4912	$15.00
U58	Stereo AM/FM radio	12482	$276.00
U69	AM/FM radio	17598	$173.00
UF1	Map light	8186	$5.00
YF5	California emissions test	3008	$15.00
YJ8	Cast aluminum wheels	4	$175.00
Z07	Off road suspension & brakes	45	$369.00

Virtually all European cars had been fitted with radial tires since the mid-1960s, but they were harder to obtain in the larger sizes fitted to American cars, including the GR70-15 which the Corvette needed. Firestone and Goodyear were proudly announced as suppliers of the revolutionary new radials for the 1973 Corvette, and each gave the impression that it alone had perfected this new technology. Firestone launched the Steel Radial 500 and Goodyear the Steelguard.

What followed was a debacle for Firestone when the Steel Radial 500 had to be recalled following numerous instances of thrown tire tread. I saw two instances of this, one front and one rear. In both, the flying tread removed the whole top of the fender above the wheel. The second case was in the early 1980s on a low-mileage car that had not heard about the recall. Even without inspecting the by now well-worn Steel Radial 500s, Firestone to their credit instantly despatched a free replacement set of new tires the same day. A black wall was base equipment, while white stripe and raised white letters were affordable and popular options.

SUSPENSION & STEERING

This was now the eleventh year that the stamped short/long arm suspension of the 1963 would be used for the Corvette, and it was still only halfway through its performing career.

Launch literature for the 1973 suggested that the shock absorbers were now stiffer as a result of the retuning of the suspension. The extra weight of the new front end would have necessitated stiffer front springs too, to restore the ride height. The rear spring had nine leaves, with no rear sway bar as standard.

The optional Z07 Off Road Suspension and Brake package was new for this year, though comprised of parts-bin components previously offered in other packages. Not available with air conditioning, and requiring either of the optional engines, it was available only with the M21 close-ratio Muncie four-speed and power brakes. Priced at $369.00, it included a $^{15}\!/_{16}$in thick front sway bar, standard anyway on the LS4 big-block, and uprated shock absorbers. The Z07 rear suspension was uprated with a stiff seven-leaf transverse spring, special shock absorbers, and a $^9\!/_{16}$in sway bar which was standard on the LS4.

BRAKES

These were unchanged for 1973, but the Z07 Off Road Suspension and Brake package now included four heavy-duty dual-pin brake calipers, as previously seen on ZR1 and ZR2. The J50 power brakes was probably required because these calipers were supplied with hard semi-metallic linings.

1974

The year 1973 had seen Corvette performance stopped in its tracks while emissions and crash survival legislation occupied the full-time working efforts of the engineers who had previously pursued power, speed and the better sports car. Now the Federal government had forced its way into the drawing office and on to the design team.

Strangely, the buying public didn't seem to mind, and the 1973 model year was the best yet. More interference was the rule for 1974, with the rear bumper now Federalized too and more power reductions, and yet the 1974 sales year would be another record.

Buyers only buy new cars they like, and the buyers were liking the new softer car very much indeed. It is easy to bemoan the lack of performance engine options that characterised the mid-1970s, but the truth was that even in 1971 more buyers wanted the base-engined car than all the optional engines put together. Compare a base-engine 1969 to the equivalent 1974 and there was no doubt which was the better car. The later car's ride on

radial tyres and cushioned body mounts was a vast improvement, and even the seats were better.

Unbelievably, the Corvette was also perceived by many as an economy car - scared by the fuel crises, many drivers were downsizing from full-size cars to similarly engined Corvettes, though many must have realized that at last here was a socially acceptable excuse to drive a Corvette for business!

BODY & BODY TRIM

The new extended 1973 nose was a major success for the Corvette so there was every reason to continue the theme. For 1974 the cast pot-metal material of the front grilles was replaced by aluminum and painted all over semi-gloss black, without the exposed chrome edge of the previous year's car. Black now replaced silver on the horizontal edges of the parking lamps to match the grilles. The bumper assembly continued as for the 1973, with the addition of a pair of transverse bracing rods to link the outer outrigger brackets to the central bumper support assembly.

Metamorphosis was completed for the 1974 model year with a new tail.

DIMENSIONS & WEIGHTS	
Length	185.5in
Width	69.2in
Height	
Sport Coupe	47.7in
Convertible	47.8in
Wheelbase	98.0in
Max track	
Front	58.7in
Rear	59.4in
Curb weight	
Sport Coupe	3390lb
Convertible	3396lb

The new tail suited the Stingray shape, a superb achievement for GM Design staff. The effect was particularly striking on the rare convertible, which was ordered by less than 12% of buyers.

COLORS

Code	Body	Suggested interior trim
910	Classic White	Black, Dark Red, Dark Blue, Neutral, Saddle, Silver
914	Silver Mist	Black, Dark Red, Dark Blue, Saddle, Silver
917	Corvette Gray	Black, Dark Red, Dark Blue, Neutral, Saddle, Silver
922	Medium Blue	Black, Dark Blue, Silver
948	Dark Green	Black, Neutral, Saddle, Silver
956	Bright Yellow	Black, Neutral, Saddle, Silver
968	Dark Brown	Black, Neutral, Saddle, Silver,
974	Medium Red	Black, Dark Red, Neutral, Saddle, Silver
976	Mille Miglia Red	Black, Dark Red, Neutral, Saddle, Silver
980	Corvette Orange	Black, Neutral, Saddle, Silver

All wheels were Argent Silver. Convertible top choice was Black or White. Custom leather interior was Black, Silver and Saddle only.

The theft alarm key switch, previously on the rear panel between the lights, was now moved to the left front fender. The key functions were changed for 1974. Since 1968 a square-headed key had been used to operate both the ignition switch and the door locks. A second oval-headed key was used for the external alarm switch, to unlock the spare wheel and to open the glovebox behind the passenger seat. Starting in 1974, the oval key was required to open the doors as well, leaving the square-headed one for the ignition only. The two-key system would survive for another generation of Corvettes until the single key returned with the 1997 C5.

1974 coupe in Corvette Orange, a new color for 1974. Soft nose and tail fascias covered extruding-bolt energy-absorbing bumper systems. Facing page: Humps over the fenders were even more accentuated by the new longer front end.

Now the Federal government required that the rear bumper be capable of withstanding a 5mph impact, just as they had insisted for the front in 1973, so the same technology was adapted to the rear of the car as well. The requirement was that the car on test could be driven backward squarely into a solid block at 5mph and then drive away without damage to lights or other safety systems such as the fuel tank and exhaust. If the car was parked and then hit by a truck at 5mph, then the effect was the same, provided that the impact was exactly square.

Just as with the front bumper described in the previous chapter, impact energy was absorbed by extruding draw bolts through a simple die

assembly. In the event of an impact the flexible urethane of the bumper cover pressed onto a rubber strip on the aluminum box-section inner bumper. In turn this forced the die down each draw bolt, dissipating the impact energy as heat. The draw bolt slider assemblies were at either end of the bumper rather than centrally as at the front, where the position was determined by the pointed nose of the car, but expensive damage was still inevitable from any impact other than the straight-on envisaged by the tidy-minded legislators. In 23 years of selling parts to repair crashed Corvettes or repairing them in my own shop I have never been asked for 'Two drawbolts

1974 gas flap was the only one with no emblem in the 35-year production run from 1962 to 1997.

and a set of Corvette rear letters, please', and I doubt if any one else has either!

To cover all this crash resisting assembly, molded polyurethane was used again. Probably because it was easier to mold, the bumper cover was made in two halves held together with aluminum rivets. The vertical seam ran between the middle letters of the Corvette name and through the license plate recess and did not look out of place.

With no bumperettes or spoilers incorporated, the 1974 tail is surely the most attractive of all the later C4 rears. On the convertible particularly, the long rear deck and smooth tail make an outstanding piece of automotive sculpture, emphasized further by the plain gas filler door, which uniquely to this year had no emblem.

CHASSIS

The frame for the 1974 was a continuation of the same old 1963 design, differing from the 1973 only in detail changes at the rear to accept the new energy-absorbing bumper system. The frame part number was stencilled on it just behind the front wheel. The second part of the VIN number was stamped on the top of the left main frame rail as usual below the driver's door, and secondly inboard of the left rear wheel on the rear frame rail.

INTERIOR

When looking for questions for the next club quiz, try this one: 'How, apart from color choices, does a 1974 Corvette interior differ from a 1973?' No hand will wave, pencils will be still. Finally someone will remember the big difference - 1974 was the year when the interior lamp changed from the long thin unit used from mid 1968 to the squarer 2in x 4in unit used until 1982. By this time someone will have remembered the other significant change - yes the rear view mirror is bigger at 10in wide, requiring narrower sun visors.

Under the dash, just to the right of the steering column on air-conditioned cars, there was a new

Lighting had to remain intact after the Federal impact test, a great excuse (right) for the stylists to recess the tail lamps and match the style of the recessed speedometer and tachometer used since 1968. The 1974 rear bumper was unique to the year (far right). It was made in two halves with a vertical split, possibly due to a lack of larger molding equipment.

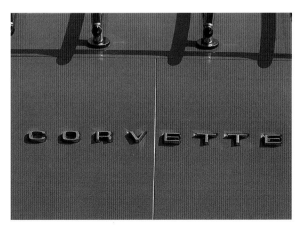

air-conditioning outlet known as a lap cooler. Behind this the ductwork was modified, which together with a deeper heel recess allowed more space for the driver's feet.

Compared with European drivers, North Americans had always been reluctant to wear the seat belts that we all knew saved lives. Sports car owners and enthusiasts recognized the benefits of seat belts and needed no persuasion to wear them, but among that unhappy majority of car drivers who didn't even like driving, the seat belts were just one more annoyance to be ignored. States were slow or unwilling to make them compulsory, so the Federal government decided to intervene directly by making 1974 cars impossible to start unless the seat belt was worn in any occupied front seat.

Although the automatic-transmission car could be started by reaching in from outside and turning the key, pressure sensors in the seats signalled the presence of occupants and disabled the cranking circuit until the relevant seat belt was buckled up. The manual transmission car required the clutch to be depressed before it would start. To simplify servicing, and for emergency use, an over-ride button was provided under the hood on the firewall to the right of the wiper motor. On the 1974 Corvette both the belt buckle and under-seat retractors were wired into the ignition interlock. Inevitably, many of these systems were quickly and easily bypassed and the law quickly forgotten. The belts were much improved by replacing the locking devices with pendulums, making the belt much easier to put on.

INSTRUMENTS & CONTROLS

Returning to that club quiz, as a bonus question for double points, what was the other significant difference between the 1973 and 1974 interior? Well, in 1973 the oil and water gauges have mainly odd number figures, while in 1974 all the numbers are even! The new electrical oil pressure gauge was now connected by wire to a sender unit located in the high-pressure oil gallery in the engine block just above the oil filter.

ENGINES

L48 350 195hp Base engine for the 1974 Corvette was again the 5.7-liter L48, which gained a nominal 5hp over the previous year's. It was effectively the 1973 engine repeated. The cylinder heads were a new cast number 333882, very similar to the base 1973 heads with a 75.47cc combustion chamber volume and 1.94in intake and 1.50in exhaust valves. This emissions head with hardened valve seats would be used for the next four years. Pistons were again dished, giving an 8.5:1 compression ratio.

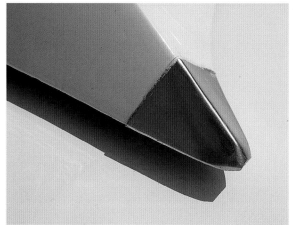

Hardtop (above) had elegant concave rear window and looked very different from the t-roofed coupe. Metal tips (left) protected the stylish rear points on the hardtop and allowed for easy vertical storage.

Option C50 rear window defroster was hidden in B-pillar on coupes, but used this elaborate duct system on convertibles.

This was the last year for the 454. A 1974 454 convertible (above) is one of the rarest Corvettes, with probably less than 1000 built. 1974 hood on a 454 (right). A rubber gasket sealed the air cleaner to the cold air duct. The cold air flap at the rear opened on hard acceleration and sounded great.

L82 350 250hp The optional L82 engine was again a carryover of the 1973 with minor changes. The cast 333882 heads were opened up for 2.02in intake and 1.60in exhaust valves, and flat-top pistons with valve reliefs gave the required 9.0:1 compression ratio.

LS4 454 270hp The LS4 big-block was a repeat of the previous year too, but this was destined to be its last year, and it lost 5hp at the same time. Shortly after he retired I met Zora Arkus-Duntov for lunch in a restaurant near the Tech Center outside Detroit. I was surprised that he and his charming wife Elfie arrived in a blue 1974 454 Corvette - perhaps I was expecting a Cadillac or something small, well engineered and foreign. He was always hard to understand, but the first thing he told me was that he liked this Corvette, it had lots of torque and great air conditioning. It was his own car and he drove it for years.

The big-block adventure was over at the end of 1974. Sales for the final year were just 3494 but this engine would go on to dominate the motorhome market, and developments of it live on in various 4x4s as well.

IDENTIFICATION

Engine block cast numbers
350cu in   3970010
454cu in   3999289

Stamped engine number suffixes
CKZ 350 195hp Rochester 4BC manual
CLA 350 195hp Rochester 4BC auto
CLB 350 195hp Rochester 4BC manual, Calif
CLC 350 195hp Rochester 4BC auto, Calif
CLD 350 250hp Rochester 4BC auto
CLH 350 250hp Rochester 4BC auto, Calif
CLR 350 250hp Rochester 4BC manual
CLS 350 250hp Rochester 4BC manual, Calif
CWM 454 270hp Rochester 4BC manual
CWR 454 270hp Rochester 4BC auto
CWS 454 270hp Rochester 4BC auto, Calif
CWT 454 270hp Rochester 4BC manual, Calif

Chassis numbers
1Z37J4S400001 through 1Z37J4S437502 (3rd digit is a 6 for convertible. 5th digit indicates engine: J=350 195hp, T=350 250hp and Z=454 270hp)

OPTIONS

Code	Option	Quantity	Price
1YZ37	Base Corvette sport coupe	32028	$6001.50
1YZ67	Base Corvette convertible	5474	$5765.50
L48	350 195hp motor	27318	$0.00
	Base four-speed wide ratio	8862	$0.00
	Base vinyl trim	12069	$0.00
	Custom Trim leather seats	19959	$154.00
A31	Power windows	23940	$86.00
A85	Shoulder harness, std with coupe	618	$41.00
C07	Auxiliary hardtop (1YZ67 only)	2612	$267.00
C08	Auxiliary top exterior vinyl trim	367	$329.00
C50	Rear window defroster	9322	$43.00
C60	Air conditioning	29397	$467.00
FE7	Gymkhana suspension	1905	$7.00
J50	Power brakes	33306	$49.00
LS4	454 270hp engine	3494	$250.00
L82	350 250hp engine	6690	$299.00
M21	Four-speed manual close ratio	3494	$0.00
M40	Turbo Hydra-Matic transmission	25146	$0.00
N37	Tilt/telescopic steering column	27700	$82.00
N41	Power-assisted steering	35944	$117.00
QRM	White stripe radials GR70 x 15	9140	$32.00
QRZ	White letter radials GR70 x 15	24102	$45.00
U05	Dual horns	5258	$4.00
U58	Stereo AM/FM radio	19581	$276.00
U69	AM/FM radio	17374	$173.00
UA1	Heavy duty battery	9169	$15.00
UF1	Map light	16101	$5.00
YF5	California emissions test	3008	$20.00
Z07	Off road suspension & brakes	47	$369.00

COOLING SYSTEM

The plastic radiator shroud was new, numbered 339175, and was used with all engines. A new white plastic coolant recovery tank numbered 339185 replaced the previous 334762.

ELECTRICS

With the new tail came new rear lamps, single-piece units capable of retaining their integrity in the rear crash test. They were unique to this year and had no visible fixings, being retained by molded-in studs. The license plate was lit by two lamps, making the 1974 the only Corvette since 1960 to have more than one.

TRANSMISSIONS

In January 1974 the familiar Muncie four-speed manual transmission was dropped in favour of a stronger Borg Warner T-10. This was an updated and strengthened version of the aluminum T-10 last seen in a Corvette in mid-1963. With a considerable drop in demand for manual transmissions, partly because the muscle car era was over and also because of the ever rising demand for automatics, General Motors decided to stop production of high-performance manual 'boxes and source them from outside instead.

The Super T-10, as it was generally known, was stronger than the Muncie, but still fully interchangeable with it, including the shifter. It had a nine-bolt side cover in contrast to the Muncie's seven bolts. In the wide-ratio M20 application the T-10 had a lower 2.64:1 first gear than the Muncie and a higher 1.33:1 third gear, an all round improvement. In the close-ratio version, first gear was 2.43:1 against the Muncie's 2.20:1 and third gear had a nice close ratio of 1.23:1.

Automatic transmission continued to be by the Turbo Hydra-Matic 400 with all engines. The choice of differential ratios was unchanged too.

WHEELS & TIRES

The wheel and tire combinations were the same as 1973's. At last the PO2 de luxe wheel covers were dropped, having sold just 1,723 sets in the previous model year. White letter tires replaced white stripes as the most popular choice.

SUSPENSION & STEERING

For 1974 a new suspension and handling package was offered in addition to the FO7. This was FE7 Gymkhana Suspension, an option which would recur through 1982. At $7.00 it was a bargain compared to the $400 ZO7 heavy-duty brake and suspension combination, and it proved immediately popular. It consisted of stiffer springs and a larger-diameter front sway bar. It did not include a rear sway bar, which was standard with the LS4 big block and included with the ZO7 package.

BRAKES

There were no changes to the braking system for 1974.

1975 & 1976

It is easy to say that 1975 marked the low point of the Corvette's development, or at least it's easy to say it until you meet the enthusiastic owner of a '75 - or set about trying to sell one. Then you start to realize the positive points, and the main one is that it is absolutely a Corvette and only about 10 per cent different to a 1970 LT1. The other plus points will become obvious as this chapter proceeds.

After the changes of the previous two years, which saw Federally required 5mph bumpers incorporated into first the front and then the rear of the car, the government were ready with another onslaught for 1975. These measures, it seemed to us at the time, would be fatal to both the Corvette as the ultimate American V8 performance car, and to Camaros, Trans-Ams and the other survivors of the muscle car era. We could also see that the Cadillacs or Lincolns we might hope to find sharing garage space with our Corvettes when we finally retired might be doomed as well.

The catalytic converter was chosen by General Motors as the first fix to meet the steep emissions requirements for 1975 model cars. We knew there were more efficient alternatives such as lean burn and fuel injection as well as rumors of developments such as stratified charge, but we also knew that none of these could be made workable in the time made available. So the dual exhaust converged into a Y-pipe, a catalytic converter was inserted behind it, and then there was another Y-pipe - thus the visual illusion of the performance exhaust was preserved.

The effect on performance was devastating. The power output of the 1975 L48 base engine was 165hp, down 30hp from 1974, the lowest since the 155hp straight six of 1955 and the lowest ever for a Corvette V8. There was no alternate engine capacity because the big-block, first seen as a 396 in 1965, was now dropped as a Corvette option. Far from ceasing production, however, it would go on to become the pre-eminent engine for powering the increasingly popular class-A motorhomes, where its massive torque at low revs was really appreciated, in the specialist chassis which Chevrolet supplied.

1975 was the last year for the C3 convertible and - we thought then - the end of convertibles forever. Ten years later the Corvette convertible would return. The author blames a decade of long hair.

DIMENSIONS & WEIGHTS 1975

Length	185.2in
Width	69.2in
Height	
Sport Coupe	48.1in
Convertible	48.2in
Wheelbase	98.0in
Max track	
Front	58.7in
Rear	59.4in
Curb weight	
Sport Coupe	3529lb
Convertible	3542lb

Despite all this, the 1975 was the best selling Corvette ever, with more than 38,000 of the fiberglass beauties produced in 10 months. The 1969 had sold about 300 cars more, but that model year ran for 13 months. 1976 sales were up again to over 46,000. All Corvettes were then and are still today built to customer order, so the build quantity is a direct reflection of customer demand. If the demand was greater than the capacity of the plant to meet orders - and there is every reason to believe that it usually was - then customers were persuaded to make their order for the following model year, or buy a used or demonstrator car from the dealer instead.

Each car built reflected customer preference in its choice of options too. While a good salesman would steer a buyer towards extra options, the final built car was still a record of that customer's aspirations and a social document of the era. General Motors is often said to be a corporation run by accountants, and although it is sad that Chevrolet made 1975 the last year for the convertible, the company was only responding to the orders it received. Despite being the cheapest Stingray one could buy, the soft top sold only 4629 units in 1975 – a decline to 12% of the total against 15% in 1974. Now of course these soft tops are by far the most valuable 1975s, not just because they are scarce but also because the fashion has returned to roadsters.

Colors chosen then were equally fascinating. Most people assume that red has always been the most popular Corvette color, but prior to the new C4 in 1984 it was only ever the top color in 1956 and 1964. Color quantities are not available for 1969-70 or 1973-74 but because red was not popular in the adjacent years, it is safe to say that it never was for the 1968-1982 C3 period. By now the majority of these cars have been refinished and red is surely the most popular color for a repaint – influenced by Woody Allen or Prince according to the owner's age.

At the time of writing white is the hardest color to sell as a used car, and the paint shops are busy painting white cars yellow, Millennium Yellow being the hot color for 2000 and 2001 Corvettes.

Nose and tail now had small black bumperettes (above). The inside structure was changed, with hydraulic absorbers at the rear to increase crash resistance. 1976 was identical to 1975 in front view (facing page). Grilles were now plastic and shorter than the metal ones used 1973-74.

COLORS 1975

Code	Body	Quantity	Suggested interior trim
10	Classic White	8007	Black, Dark Red, Dark blue, Neutral, Medium Saddle, Silver
13	Silver	4710	Black, Dark Red, Dark Blue, Medium Saddle, Silver
22	Bright Blue	2869	Black, Dark Blue, Silver
27	Steel Blue	1268	Black, Dark Blue, Silver
42	Bright Green	1664	Black, Neutral, Medium Saddle, Silver
56	Bright Yellow	2883	Black, Neutral, Medium Saddle
67	Medium Saddle	3403	Black, Neutral, Medium Saddle
70	Orange Flame	3030	Black, Neutral, Medium Saddle
74	Dark Red	3342	Black, Dark Red, Neutral, Medium Saddle, Silver
76	Mille Miglia Red	3355	Black, Dark Red, Neutral, Medium Saddle, Silver

All wheels were Argent Silver. Convertible top choice was Black or White. Custom leather interior was Black, Silver, Dark Blue, Medium Saddle and Dark Red.

For 1975 and 1976, however, Classic White was by far the most ordered finish, and this would continue for the next year, an astonishing contrast to the somber dark greens which topped the list in the late 1960s.

Confounding the experts and the technical press, the Corvette was selling very well despite the loss of performance. So it is clear that the mid-'70s Corvette was delivering much more than just performance, and this rising sales trend would continue until the end of the decade. This was the era of the 'double nickel' 55mph national speed limit, an age which had already seen a first fuel crisis; the Corvette was quiet, comfortable and economical at this speed and could reach it in under six seconds from a standing start. Appearance and the selfish appeal of the two-seater were probably the factors that were selling the Stingray all along, and they are undoubtedly what attracts people to them today.

BODY & BODY TRIM

Both the front and rear soft bumper fascias were restyled for 1975 to cover newly designed inner bumper assemblies. The front bumper incorporated new black-painted overriders on either side of the license plate. These covered stiff rubber buffers which were the first stage of the new energy-absorbing bumper system, which no longer used the extruding bolts of the 1973-74 system. A honeycomb polyurethane absorber was mounted behind the fascia on either side, attached to a support bolted to a main tubular crossbar which was also used as a vacuum reservoir for the headlight actuators.

While the 1973-74 grilles were metal, the 1975 units were now plastic and shorter too. The combination turn signal and parking lamp was the same unit as the previous year's, but had different part numbers.

At the rear the bumper fascia unit was also new. It was now in one piece and had small overriders at the outer ends to match those on the front. The new shape was required to cover an entirely new

DIMENSIONS & WEIGHTS 1976	
Length	185.2in
Width	69.2in
Height	48.0in
Wheelbase	98.0in
Max track	
Front	58.7In
Rear	59.4in
Curb weight	3541lb

COLORS 1976

Code	Body	Quantity	Suggested interior trim
10	Classic White	10764	Black, Blue-green, Buckskin, Dark blue, Firethorn, Smoked Gray, White
13	Silver	6934	Black, Blue-green, Buckskin, Firethorn, Smoked Gray, White
22	Bright Blue	3268	Black, Smoked Gray
33	Dark Green	2038	Black, Blue-green, Buckskin, Smoked Gray, White
37	Mahogany	4182	Black, Buckskin, Firethorn, Smoked Gray, White
56	Bright Yellow	3389	Black, Dark Blue
64	Buckskin	2954	Black, Buckskin, Dark Blue, Firethorn, White
69	Dark brown	4447	Black, Buckskin, Dark Blue, White
70	Orange Flame	4073	Black, Buckskin, Dark Blue
72	Red	4590	Black, Buckskin, Firethorn, Smoked Gray, White

All wheels were Argent Silver.
Custom leather interior was Black, Blue-green, Buckskin, Dark Blue, White, Firethorn, Smoked Gray.

A record 46,558 Corvettes were sold in 1976 and White was by far the most popular color.

crash absorber system. This used an inner bar assembly which mounted onto oil-filled shock absorbers designed to take the rear impact. It should not be imagined that leaning against the rear bumper would eventually compress the absorber. Indeed, the optional trailer package offered from 1977 actually bolted to the impact bar and all towing forces were taken through the two hydraulic absorber units.

The color of the bumper fascias often varied considerably from the main body, because these units were painted separately from the body and with a paint which contained a flex agent. The mismatch progressively worsened with time as fading took effect too. The later one-piece tail is often seen fitted to 1974s, but is not a direct substitute as much cutting away of the inner structure is required to achieve a fit.

Cloisonné emblem (above) lost its outside lettering for 1975, and a similar emblem was now fitted to the gas filler lid (left). Additional sticker warned against leaded gas, which could damage the catalytic converter introduced for 1975. Early 1976 small rear emblem (below) fitted into a molded recess. Later bumper had no recess and a larger emblem used through 1979.

Black vinyl was always an option for the 1968-76 hardtop.

The front emblem was a similar red cloisonné design to that first seen on the 1973. For 1975 it had the words 'Chevrolet Motor Division' and 'Corvette' around the central red starburst, while for 1976 it only had 'Corvette'.

A smaller matching design without the outside lettering was used on both years' gas filler cap lids. Because unleaded gas was now mandatory an 'Unleaded Gas Only' clear Mylar sticker was affixed to the lower edge of the lid. The filler neck itself was now the restricted-size unleaded type too, ending a 12-year tradition of 4in filler necks which would take a racing size filler for faster pit stops and allowed manual cleaning but more practically allowed visual inspection of the fuel available when the gauge became untrustworthy.

The rear emblem for the 1975 had the same individual Corvette letters as the 1974, set into matched recesses in the polyurethane. This changed for 1976 with a new script emblem, which also fitted into a matched recess in early production cars. Later the emblem was larger, surface fitted to the bumper, and the same as used through 1979.

The 1975 hood panel was externally the same as the 1973-74 and incorporated the same cold air induction system, drawing cold air from the high pressure area at the base of the windshield. For 1976 a new air cleaner system drew cold air from a duct arrangement which led to the front of the radiator, but the external design of the hood panel remained unchanged. Now that the big-block was gone, the optional L82 was celebrated with an L82 emblem when fitted.

Vent grilles had been a feature of the rear deck since 1968 and were part of the Astro-Ventilation through-ventilation system. When air conditioning was fitted they were blocked off, and when fitted to the convertible it was possible to see right through them because the Astro outlet was vertical in the rear bulkhead on that model. For 1976 Astro-Ventilation was discontinued and the grilles went too.

The chassis was effectively unchanged from 1963 and was used for 20 years of production. This restored chassis looks great - too nice to cover with a body. Fitting the front and rear crash bumpers makes the car much longer.

CHASSIS

The 1975 and 1976 chassis were effectively continuations of the 1974, with different holes or the bumper attachments, and still using a detachable transmission crossmember when automatic transmission was fitted. Despite the Y-piped exhaust both exhaust pipe holes were still present and would remain so until 1980, making the retrofit of a dual exhaust a simple matter.

INTERIOR

The 1975 interior was really more of the same, with Medium Saddle replacing the Silver of 1974. The 1976 model year, however, saw the introduction of some dramatic new color combinations, based on White. When this was ordered as the interior color, then the carpets, dash and seat belts were keyed to the exterior color. If White seats were ordered with a White car, then the carpets, door panels and belts could be Black, Blue-Green or Dark Firethorn. The other car colors drew the carpet, dash and belts as follows when White was ordered for the seats: Silver

Metallic/Smoke Gray, Dark Green Metallic/Blue-Green, Mahogany Metallic/Dark Firethorn, Light Buckskin/Dark Brown, Dark Brown Metallic/Dark Brown, Corvette Red/Dark Firethorn. These were the most interesting interiors and never fail to surprise the most jaded expert, who suddenly realises that what he assumed was a home-brewed re-trim in a lowly '76 is actually original and correct and looks great too.

INSTRUMENTS & CONTROLS

Because the new-for-1975 HEI distributor had no provision for a mechanical tachometer drive, a new electronic tachometer was fitted in place of the previous cable-driven instrument. After years of worn drive gears in the distributor Chevrolet had the chance to give the Corvette a reliable engine speed display device – and missed it. Tens of millions of cars are built every year with completely reliable electronic tachs, but we got the dud. The 1975-82 tachometer indicates 1500rpm with the engine off and the needle dives down to the true idle rpm once the engine starts. Failures were common within five years from new, and the needle would often inexplicably stick at 6000rpm. It took almost 20 years for a reliable $95 replacement circuit board to appear on the market and fix this unnecessary problem. The reason for the problem was outlined at the very beginning in the June/July 1975 issue of *Corvette News*. In designing the tachometer, it said, the engineers had taken a 90°

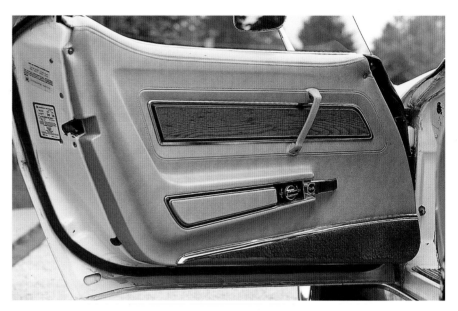

1976 Custom Interior door panel (above) with 'wood grain accent' and carpeted scuff strip. Door lock knob and release handle (left). 1976 with Buckskin Custom Interior Trim (below).

Some didn't like the 1976 Corvette using a steering wheel from a lowlier GM car, but it was smaller, more comfortable and matched the interior color. 1976 auto shift console (right). 1969 to 1976 heater and air conditioning control was always hard to read.

fuel gauge core and added circuitry to increase the deflection of the needle to 310° to match the speedometer. Happily this kind of design is exceptional in the history of the Corvette.

Three tachometer faces were supplied, redlined for the base L48 engine at 5300rpm, for the L82 with C60 air conditioning at 5600rpm, and for the L82 without C60 at 6000rpm. The speedometer was given an inner ring of kilometer figures for 1975.

1975 was the last year for thin black-rimmed 15in steering wheel which had seemed very up to date back in 1969. A new steering wheel was fitted for 1976. Much derided as a cheap borrowing from the humble four-cylinder Vega, it was a definite improvement over the thin 1969-75 wheel. With two cross spokes, it had a smaller but fatter rim of 14in diameter, but best of all it was color co-ordinated to the interior for the first time since 1963. The telescopic adjustment, when specified, was by a plain knurled ring directly behind the horn. It is commonly believed that this was a 1976-only steering wheel, but it was definitely also used on those few 1977-79 cars which were ordered without a tilt and telescopic column.

Power brakes were still optional in 1976, but they were fitted to all cars built. As a rule disc brakes on Corvettes have always felt better if power assisted, particularly on automatic cars, while the fairly heavy clutch on manual transmission cars was well matched to an unassisted brake pedal. Now there would be no choice. This was also the last year for optional power steering, with just 173 opting for steering the hard way. The system, which dated from the late 1950s and had not changed since 1963, can easily be added to improve any 1968-76 Corvette not so equipped.

ENGINES

Today's Corvette has the same size engine as the 1975 but it develops 345 horsepower, more than twice the 165 horsepower of the L48. The engine's emissions are so clean that in a city the air behind the LS1-powered car is probably cleaner than the air in front of it, and yet it will go more than 50 per cent further than the L48 on a gallon of gas at 75mph on the highway. So, in looking at the lowly 1975, remember that this engine, which initially seemed like a victory for a car-hating legislature, was the beginning of a cycle of improvement, still continuing today, in which power, emissions and fuel economy have only got better

L48 165hp The base L48 motor still breathed through the same cold air induction system as the 1974 and the carburetor was the usual Rochester Quadrajet, now numbered 7045222 automatic and 7045223 manual. As with all years since 1968, the fourth numeral of the Rochester carburetor stamped number indicated the model year.

IDENTIFICATION 1975			
Engine block cast numbers			
350 cu in		3970010	
Stamped engine number suffixes			
CHA	350	165hp	Rochester 4BC manual
CHB	350	165hp	Rochester 4BC auto
CHC	350	205hp	Rochester 4BC manual
CHR	350	205hp	Rochester 4BC auto, Calif
CHU	350	165hp	Rochester 4BC manual
CHZ	350	165hp	Rochester 4BC auto, Calif
CKC	350	205hp	Rochester 4BC, auto
CRJ	350	165hp	Rochester 4BC manual
CRK	350	165hp	Rochester 4BC auto
CRL	350	205hp	Rochester 4BC manual
CRM	350	205hp	Rochester 4BC, auto
CUA	350	165hp	Rochester 4BC, manual
CUB	350	165hp	Rochester 4BC, manual
CUB	350	205hp	Rochester 4BC, manual
CUT	350	205hp	Rochester 4BC manual

Chassis numbers
1Z37J5S400001 through 1Z37J5S438465 (3rd digit is a 6 for convertible. 5th digit indicates engine: J=350 165hp, T=350 205hp)

An unrestored 1975 L48 such as this is fascinating to the restorer, and the NCRS Bow Tie awards program encourages preservation, not restoration, of very original cars like this. Spaghetti of hoses mainly relates to emissions equipment. At 165hp, the 1975 was the lowest rated V8 ever fitted to a Corvette, but for the next 25 years power would only go up – so the 1975 was at least the beginning of something good.

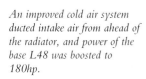

An improved cold air system ducted intake air from ahead of the radiator, and power of the base L48 was boosted to 180hp.

IDENTIFICATION 1976

Engine block cast numbers
350cu in   3970010

Stamped engine number suffixes
CHC   350 210hp   Rochester 4BC manual
CKC   350 210hp   Rochester 4BC auto
CKW   350 180hp   Rochester 4BC manual
CKX   350 180hp   Rochester 4BC auto
CLS   350 180hp   Rochester 4BC manual, Calif

Chassis numbers
1Z37L6S400001 through 1Z37L6S446558 (5th digit indicates engine: L=350 180hp, X=350 210hp)

The cast iron 346249 intake manifold was common to both L48 and L82 engines and was very similar to the 1974 340261. It was used on all engines through 1977. The cylinder heads were cast 333882 and were also used on the L82, as in the previous year. Valve size was 1.94in intake and 1.50in exhaust. The pistons for the base 165 horsepower engine were cast aluminum, with a dished crown and yielding an 8.5:1 compression ratio. The cast crankshaft rotated in two-bolt main bearings in the now-usual 3970010 cylinder block.

The camshaft was the same cast number 3896930 that had been used since 1971, and as everything else was the same as the 195hp 1974 engine it is clear that a full 30hp was missing somewhere. Of course, it was the restrictive catalytic converter that was taking the power, combined with the effectively single exhaust system and the leaner mixture, which required the extra power of the HEI distributor to fire it.

L82 205hp An additional 40hp was available by spending an extra $336.00 to get the L82 engine, which was a massive 45hp down on the 1974 version of the same motor. Like its sibling it was suffering from the effects of the catalyst, which had an even greater effect on the more powerful engine despite the provision of a 2⅛in rather than a 2in exhaust system.

It was different from the L48 in the following respects. The Quadrajet carburetor was numbered 70452210 automatic and 7045211 manual, and was jetted to deliver a little more power. The valves were bigger at 2.02in intake and 1.60in exhaust, while forged flat-top pistons with a valve relief raised the compression ratio to 9.0:1. Connecting rods were selected, heat treated, shot-peened and magnafluxed. The crankshaft was forged instead of cast, and carried the cast mark 330550. Main bearing caps were 4-bolt and the crankshaft harmonic balancer was of 8in diameter rather than the 6in unit of the L48.

Still comparing the unrestricted 1974 motors to the catalysed 1975 units, it should be noted that the peak power on the '75s was developed at much lower revs. The L48's peak power point was 4400rpm in 1974 and only 3800rpm in 1975, while the L82's peak power point went down from 5200rpm to 4800rpm.

Happily, today we can bolt on a pair of high-compression aluminum heads, fit a livelier cam and a dual exhaust - with twin low-restriction cats if required by local laws - and restore the power output back to late-1960s levels or beyond.

For 1976 a new cold air induction system came to the rescue. With bigger ducts than the in-hood system used since 1973, this took cold and hopefully pressurized air from in front of the radiator and contributed to slightly increased power at higher revs. The L48 now made 180hp at 4000rpm and the L82 210hp at 5200rpm. The latter was now prohibited in California because its emissions performance could not meet that state's stricter rules, and the manual transmission was banned too.

COOLING SYSTEM

Radiators were all copper, with a coolant recovery system via a plastic bottle on the right-hand inner fender. These engines with their lower outputs were never demanding on the cooling system.

EMISSION SYSTEM

Since 1968 AIR pumps had been fitted to most Corvettes but, as in 1974, there was another exception in 1975 for base-engined cars fitted with the Turbo Hydra-Matic 400 transmission. All other cars for 1975 and 1976 were fitted with AIR pumps.

OPTIONS 1975			
Code	Option	Quantity	Price
1YZ37	Base Corvette Sport Coupe	33836	$6810.10
1YZ67	Base Corvette Convertible	4629	$6550.10
	Base L48 350 165hp motor	36093	$0.00
	Base four-speed wide ratio	8935	$0.00
	Base vinyl trim	-	$0.00
	Custom Trim leather seats	-	$154.00
A31	Power windows	28745	$93.00
A85	Shoulder harness, std with coupe	646	$41.00
C07	Auxiliary Hardtop (1YZ67 only)	2407	$267.00
C08	Auxiliary top with vinyl trim	279	$350.00
C50	Rear window defroster	13760	$46.00
C60	Air conditioning	31914	$490.00
FE7	Gymkhana suspension	3194	$7.00
J50	Power brakes	35842	$50.00
L82	350 205hp engine	2372	$336.00
M21	Four-speed manual close ratio	1057	$0.00
M40	Turbo Hydra-Matic transmission	28473	$0.00
N37	Tilt/telescopic steering column	31830	$82.00
N41	Power-assisted steering	37591	129.00
QRM	White stripe radials GR70 x 15	5233	$35.00
QRZ	White letter radials GR70 x 15	30407	$48.00
U05	Dual horns	22011	$4.00
U58	Stereo AM/FM radio	24701	$284.00
U69	AM/FM radio	12902	$178.00
UA1	Heavy duty battery	16778	$15.00
UF1	Map light	21676	$5.00
YF5	California emissions test	3037	$20.00
Z07	Off road suspension & brakes	144	$400.00

As in the previous two years an evaporative control system was fitted, the principal element being the carbon canister mounted in the inner fender behind the driver's side front wheel. The catalytic converter was the big news for 1975, and this device was placed under the car approximately under the passenger seat. All Corvettes would be fitted with converters from this point forward. The 1975-76 units were the biggest and heaviest ever made, and unfortunately the least free-flowing too.

ELECTRICS

The High Energy Ignition - HEI - distributor was an all-new product, and many millions were fitted to General Motors cars during 1975. Although bigger

VIN number, build date and tire information stickers. At last GM realized that their chassis, from 1963, handled better with more air in the back tires than the front.

Far left: Restored 1975 L48. Left: Rear suspension – the diagonal brace was added for the 1969 model year. The front suspension (above) used upper arms and knuckles from late '60s full-size Chevrolets.

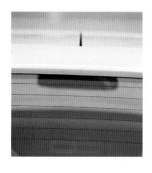

1976 was the last year of the U51 mirror-mounted map light (above), introduced in 1973. An optional heated wire defogger (below)replaced the fan blower defroster in 1976.

than the contact breaker type unit it replaced, it incorporated the previously separate coil and gave twice the voltage too. In that great way that GM have, they made it with the same fitting as the old unit so that this neat self-contained unit could retrofit any number of old hot-rods and racing cars. Its ability to fire on next to no volts was legendary. This was not the first Corvette breakerless ignition: K66 Transistor Ignition, which had been around since 1964, was mandatory on some engines and was last used in 1969.

TRANSMISSIONS

The base transmission was now the four-speed Borg Warner Super T-10, although the automatic was a no-cost and more popular option. The main case casting number was 1304 065903 and the extension housing 1304 066901 for both years. Input and output spline count was 26/32. First gear was 2.64:1 This was available with both engines, while the wide-ratio version with 2.43:1 first gear was offered as a no-cost option with the L82 engine only.

The automatic transmission was once again the superb Turbo Hydra-Matic 400. For both years this was a no-cost option with the L48 motor but an extra-cost option when ordered with the L82. Quite why it was worth an extra $120 in 1975 is unexplained - except by General Motors' unerring ability to earn extra profit with options - but in 1976 the Turbo Hydra-Matic 350 became the base automatic transmission and the 400 was supplied only with the L82. The superior product was undoubtedly worth the extra $134.

The differential choice for 1975 was the same as for the previous three years and marked the last year for the ¼-miler's favorite 4.11: 1. Interestingly, the author's favorite 2.73:1 ratio of 1968-70 was also reprised for 1975 only. With a non air conditioned automatic L82 redlined at 6000rpm, that would give a theoretical top speed of 175mph - unfortunately not possible on 205hp. In 1976 the choice was just 3.08:1, 3.36:1, 3.55:1 or 3.70:1.

WHEELS & TIRES

Half way through their reign as the all-time most popular Corvette wheel, the 8.5 x 15 Rally wheels were the only option for 1975. Eventually they would be fitted to almost 350,000 cars: with five fitted to each car until 1977 and four thereafter, that's more than two million wheels.

The much delayed launch of the YJ8 aluminum wheels came in 1976. With eight slots, they were a better looking alternative to the popular five-slot aftermarket wheels fitted to so many cars in the early '70s, and saved a useful 8lb unsprung weight per wheel. They were made in Mexico by Kelsey Hayes and these markings were cast on the back of each wheel. The slots were painted black and the wheel was clear coated. Only four were supplied per car, the spare being a standard Rally wheel.

The base tire was a blackwall Goodyear Steelgard or a Firestone Steel Radial 500, the latter the same tire fitted and subsequently recalled since 1973. White lettered and ⅜in white striped tires were optional, supplied by either Goodyear or Firestone.

SUSPENSION & STEERING

Ten-leaf springs replaced the nine leaf items as the stock rear suspension medium for 1975 and the rear strut rods were made larger to accommodate larger bushes. There were no changes at the front. The Z07 optional performance suspension continued as for the previous two years, with heavy-duty shock absorbers, stiffer front springs, a seven-leaf rear spring, a rear sway bar and thicker front sway bar. This option was only available with close-ratio M21 transmission and the L-82 engine, and included two-pin heavy-duty brake calipers. Optional FE7 Gymkhana suspension replaced the Z07 package for 1976 and the engine and transmission restrictions were dropped, along with the heavy-duty brakes.

BRAKES

Brakes were unchanged except that the heavy-duty two-pin calipers that were part of the Z07 option in 1975 were dropped from the Gymkhana suspension of 1976.

OPTIONS 1976

Code	Option	Quantity	Price
1YZ37	Base Corvette Sport Coupe	46558	$7604.85
L48	Base 350 165hp motor	40838	$0.00
	Base four-speed wide ratio	7845	$0.00
	Base vinyl trim	-	$0.00
	Custom Trim leather seats	-	$164.00
A31	Power windows	38700	$107.00
C49	Rear window defogger	24960	$78.00
C60	Air conditioning	40787	$523.00
FE7	Gymkhana suspension	5368	$35.00
J50	Power brakes, required	46558	$59.00
L82	350 210hp engine	5720	$481.00
M21	Four-speed manual close ratio	2088	$0.00
M40	Turbo Hydra-Matic transmission	36625	$134.0
N37	Tilt/telescopic steering column	41797	$95.00
N41	Power-assisted steering	46385	$151.00
QRM	White stripe radials GR70 x 15	3992	$37.00
QRZ	White letter radials GR70 x 15	39923	$51.00
U58	Stereo AM/FM radio	34272	$281.00
U69	AM/FM radio	11083	$187.00
UA1	Heavy duty battery	25909	$16.00
UF1	Map light	35361	$10.00
YF5	California emissions test	3527	$50.00
YJ8	Aluminum wheels	6253	$299.00

1977

The rise and rise of Corvette sales had continued through 1975 and 1976 with production for the latter more than double that of the 1971 five years earlier. The Corvette had shed most of its muscle-car options, assumed a personal car image and was selling like never before.

Now for 1977 changes were made that proved that once again the Corvette was benefiting from development that was aimed at satisfying the owner and driver instead of the Federal government.

The option list was allowed to grow again, even if some of the new offerings were an unexciting trailer hitch and cruise control that had been available on Cadillacs for more than a decade. Sport mirrors were a big improvement, but the proposed transparent CC1 'moon roofs' were dropped after the manufacturers felt that they could not be tied by GM's exclusivity agreement.

The half millionth Corvette was built on March 15 1977, almost 24 years after the first one rolled off the temporary assembly line in Flint, Michigan. Like that first car, it was Classic White, the third consecutive year that this was the most popular color. It would take just 15 more years to build the millionth car on July 2 1992.

Bill Mitchell retired in 1977. Mitchell had joined General Motors in December 1935 and within a year was chief designer of the Cadillac Studio. He was made Director of Styling in 1954 and Vice President, Styling in 1958. By building and then racing his unique Sting Ray racer in that year he

shaped the future of the Corvette, because it was this shape that was developed into the first 1963 Sting Ray. Like a larger than life orchestral conductor, he led and inspired his design team to create the great GM automotive shapes of the era, and then persuaded his fellow board members to build them. In 1972 he had GM Styling renamed GM Design Staff.

On his retirement the Stingray name was dropped, surely more than a coincidence after his years of promoting the virtues of deep sea fish. One of his design team, Chuck Jordan, was appointed head of Styling Staff in his place.

BODY & EXTERNAL TRIM

The expensive and now rather dated cloisonné front nose and rear gas tank emblems were dropped in favor of a new simple stretched variation of the traditional crossed flags, an effective and instant update of the car with a few dollars worth of well designed but cheap badges.

The hood panel now lost its rear central grille too, reflecting the disappearance of the cold air hood duct the previous year, and its replacement by the duct system over the radiator. The hood panel release system was also new and simplified, with a hook and bar replacing the previous plunger and latch system. The cross cable and latches were now on the bulkhead where they were previously on the hood panel itself.

1977 saw record sales of 49,213 of the now rather aged design, and the half millionth was built on March 15 1977. The Stingray name was dropped: now this was just a Corvette.

New extended crossed-flag emblems were added to the 1977 fenders during production. Early 1977s have no emblems on the fenders.

1977 gas filler.

Twin Sport Mirrors painted body color were a welcome new option and the YJ8 eight-slot aluminum wheels introduced for 1976 saved weight and looked great.

The Stingray script was now missing from the front fender and for early production the panel was blank. Then an extended crossed flag to match the front and rear emblems was added to either side of the car. Late in production, July 1977, the lock for the alarm moved from the front left fender to be integrated with the door key.

A change in the filler material used over the front and rear fender bonding strips led to premature sinkage of the paint in these areas, most noticeable on cars with metallic paint finishes. This was initially a cause for concern, but is better appreciated as a sign of an original and unpainted car. The problem persisted through the next two years, but was most pronounced on the 1977.

COLORS

Code	Body	Quantity	Suggested interior trim
10	Classic White	9408	Black, Blue, Buckskin, Brown, Red, Smoked Gray, White
13	Silver	6934	Black, Blue, Red, Smoked Gray, White
19	Black	6070	Black, Buckskin, Red, Smoked Gray, White
26	Light Blue	5967	Black, Smoked Gray, White
28	Dark Blue	2038	Black, Blue, Buckskin, Smoked Gray, White
52	Yellow	71	Black, Brown
56	Bright Yellow	1942	Black, Brown
66	Orange	4012	Black, Brown, Buckskin
80	Tan	4588	Black, Buckskin, Brown, Red, White
72	Medium Red	4057	Black, Buckskin, Red, Smoked Gray, White
83	Dark Red	3434	Black, Buckskin, Smoked Gray

All wheels were Argent Silver.

CHASSIS

The chassis was effectively identical with that of the 1975 and would run unchanged through 1979.

INTERIOR

While a whole new interior package was planned for 1978, some of those changes were introduced early for this year. Thus 1977 became something of a transitional year. The trim around the roof pillars and targa roofs had always been a composite of colored textured vinyl on a foam core, but now these were replaced by simple grained molded hard plastic. The effect was good and the cost saving no doubt considerable. These hard trims were more durable as well as more easily cleaned. They were a particular improvement at the inside top of the windshield pillars where, unlike the previous foam-filled trims, they did not suffer damage from the targa roof latches.

The 1977 sun visors were mounted to a swivel so that they could protect from sun shining in the side windows too.

INSTRUMENTS

A new steering wheel was the dominant change for the driver in 1977. The three spokes were brushed stainless steel, with the central lower spoke extended under and tack welded to the boss for extra strength.

Leather to match the interior color was stitched over a durable foam rubber rim. Though found in more than 90 per cent of this year's cars, the new wheel was part of the $165 N37 tilt/tele steering column option. For those cars with the regular steering column, a four-spoke wheel very like the 1976 was used.

Another major and well overdue change was the shortening of the steering column by two inches, allowing a better driving position. The 1977 column has a unique multi-purpose turn signal stalk, also combining the functions of windshield wash and wipe and headlight dimmer. Previous wiper switches were on the dash in the very center of the car, and dimmer switches on the floor, hidden under the carpet, to be operated by the left foot. Saginaw Steering's attempt to combine the functions into one lever were inept. Stalks that were not broken by a slight encounter with a left knee wore out and fell apart anyway, due to inadequate design and poor materials. This author's Corvette parts career started in 1977 and the stalks and pivots were the biggest sellers for that year's new cars.

The dimmer switch sensibly remained on the turn signal stalk and the wiper control migrated across to the left side of the dash the following year. Cruise control was a new option for 1977, a vacuum mechanical system with a module driven by the speedometer cable. A press button on the tilt stalk engaged the desired constant speed, and a dab of the brake pedal canceled it. It was only available with automatic transmission and tilt/telescopic steering. The cruise control was one of those markers that showed that the Corvette was becoming a more of a personal luxury car and less of a sports car. After all, cruise control was not a new invention but had been an option on full-size Chevrolets for the previous ten years, though the Cruise Master system was a new system for 1977.

Since 1963 Corvettes had been fitted with unique radios, great looking receivers which were integrated with the interior design of the cabin. The much cheaper full-size Chevrolet sedans, Monte Carlos and Chevelles had been offered with an AM/FM 8-track tape player since 1972, and for five years Corvette owners had been denied the right to play their own music as they drove. But now there was a rationalization and the diecast five-clock center instrument cluster bezel went out in favor of a new black plastic cluster unit designed to accommodate the range of the Corporation's in-car entertainment systems. The small gauges were of a new design with thin bright red needles with chrome bosses. The ammeter was replaced by a voltmeter for 1977. The styling of the new cluster included allen head screws round each gauge, giving a nice high-tech impression that each gauge could be removed from the front. Sadly the screw heads were fake and just part of the plastic molding.

The new steering wheel (above) was leather wrapped and color matched to the interior. Non-tilt cars continued with the 1976 four-spoke wheel. All 1977s had Custom Interior trim as standard. Cloth seat inserts could be ordered in place of leather and the door trim plate (left) was now finished in black.

The dimmer switch was moved from the floor and combined with the wiper and washer control on the turn signal stalk. This arrangement was not satisfactory, and the wipers would get their own switch again in 1978.

IDENTIFICATION

Engine block cast numbers
350cu in   3970010

Stamped engine number suffixes
CHD   350 180hp   Rochester 4BC auto, Calif
CKD   350 180hp   Rochester 4BC auto, altitude
CKZ   350 180hp   Rochester 4BC manual
CLA   350 180hp   Rochester 4BC auto
CLB   350 180hp   Rochester 4BC auto, altitude
CLC   350 180hp   Rochester 4BC auto, Calif
CLD   350 210hp   Rochester 4BC manual
CLF   350 210hp   Rochester 4BC auto

Chassis numbers
1Z37L7S400001 through 1Z37L7S449213 (5th digit indicates engine: L=350 180hp, X=350 210hp.)

Classic parking brake lever still operated inadequate drum and shoes inside rear discs.

New center console was all plastic, with fake Allen screw heads molded into the face. It would take the standard range of GM radios and eight-track tape players.

Wood and wood accents were finally banished from the Corvette. The new shift console was black plastic and did not carry the motor specifications.

The 1977 L48 engine was painted Corporate Blue.

DIMENSIONS & WEIGHTS

Length	185.2in
Width	69.2in
Height	48.0in
Wheelbase	98.0in
Max track	
Front	58.7in
Rear	59.4in
Curb weight	3534lb

The shift surround console, previously diecast metal, was now plastic too, and the traditional thumb-wheel controls for the heating and optional air conditioning were replaced by a pair of more reliable levers. The automatic gearshift boot was changed to leather to match the manual boot, in place of the plastic slider used previously.

Electric window switches, when fitted, were included in this panel. The easily broken hard plastic parking brake console was replaced by a color-matched cushioned vinyl center armrest, which was slotted for the parking brake. It was never clear why this console had not been padded since 1968. One of the most popular aftermarket accessories for the previous cars was a T-cushion, which covered the hard plastic console and was cleverly retained by a T-shaped extension hooked between the seats.

ENGINES

The big change under the hood for 1977 was that from very early in the production run, at about car 3000, the engine was painted GM Corporate Blue instead of Chevy Orange. Otherwise there were no significant changes. Both the 180hp base L48 and optional 210hp L82 continued just as before.

The idle stop solenoid, used to completely close the throttle in 1975 and 1976, was now rewired to increase idle speed during air conditioning operation if this option was fitted, perhaps because the axial compressor introduced late in 1976 production used more power at low revs.

That's it? Yes, and compare this paragraph with the same one in Chapter 3 in which we had five optional engines, four of them 427s. But the 'Vette was still alive, past the crash test and emissions hurdles and selling more cars than ever. The press had predicted that by now the powerplant would be a V6 or even a Wankel rotary, and yet we still had the best and most modifiable V8 ever built powering the best looking American car of 1977.

ELECTRICS

From time to time Corvette electrical components have been less than adequate for their intended purpose. We can remember the Borg clocks fitted from 1963, almost all the horns ever mounted in front of a radiator, and the 1975-82 tachometer, while the 1986-91 alternator and the damp-prone 1992-93 distributor were still waiting to be designed to plague future generations.

By General Motors' standards the new 1977 five-gauge center cluster was maybe not that bad because it usually survived five years and saw out the warranty, but it would start to fail soon after that. The problem was that the connections for the gauges and the dash lighting were made via a flexible copper and plastic printed circuit. The terminals of the gauges were fastened with nuts through holes in the circuit, and a multiplug engaged with the cut ends of the circuit and into a socket. The printed circuit went brittle and failed, and gauges and dash lighting failed with it. Worst of all, the replacement printed circuit, an inconsequential piece of flimsy copper and plastic film, has always cost more than $150.

The optional entertainment systems that demanded this new console with a larger aperture were a mono AM/FM radio U69, a stereo AM/FM radio U58 and, the most popular option fitted to almost half the cars built, an eight-track stereo AM/FM UM2. These were all integral units, not requiring the firewall-mounted transistor pack of the previous nine years.

The mirror-mounted optional map light was now discontinued, though there was now a focused lamp, in the top of the console to light the heater controls, which could be used as a map light. The lamp in the small center rear compartment was also deleted for 1977, as was the lamp at the back of the rear storage area, replaced by a dome light in the middle of the roof T-bar.

A new optional ZX2 convenience group was selected by more than 80 per cent of buyers. It included a dome light delay, a light warning buzzer, an under-hood light, a spare tire carrier lamp, and a vanity mirror for the passenger. A low fuel warning light was part of the package, but introduced late due to supply problems. These units are surprisingly reliable in service; as a dealer in a country where gas is five dollars a gallon, the author is very familiar with their operation!

TRANSMISSIONS

As with the motor, there were no changes to the transmission or driveline for 1977. The base automatic transmission was again the TH 350, but if an L82 was ordered with automatic then, as in 1976, the TH 400 was fitted at extra cost, now $146.

Once again the manual transmission was not available in California for emissions reasons. If the manual transmission was ordered with the L82, then the close-ratio M21 four-speed 'box was compulsory. While this might have been the optimum combination for the track, the wide-ratio M20 box was always better for the road and the restriction was strange.

WHEELS & TIRES

These continued exactly as for the previous two years. The base-equipment center cap and trim ring was gradually being displaced by the YJ8 aluminum wheels: this year they would be fitted to a full

Code	Option	Quantity	Price
	OPTIONS		
1YZ37 B	Base Corvette Sport Coupe	49213	$8647.65
L48	Base 350 180hp motor	43065	$0.00
	Base four-speed wide ratio	5922	$0.00
A31	Power windows	44341	$107.00
C49	Rear window defogger	30411	$84.00
C60	Air conditioning	45249	$553.00
D35	Sport mirrors	20206	$36.00
FE7	Gymkhana suspension	7269	$38.00
G95	Optional rear axle ratio	972	$14.00
K30	Cruise control	29161	$88.00
L82	350 210hp engine	6148	$495.00
M21	Four-speed manual close ratio	2060	$0.00
M40	Turbo Hydra-Matic transmission	41231	$0.00/$146.00
NA6	High altitude emissions	854	$22.00
N37	Tilt/telescopic steering column	46487	$165.00
QRZ	White letter radials GR70 x 15	46227	$57.00
U58	Stereo AM/FM radio	18483	$281.00
U69	AM/FM radio	4700	$187.00
UM2	Stereo AM/FM radio/8-track	24603	$414.00
UL5	Radio delete	1427	$0.00
UA1	Heavy duty battery	32882	$17.00
V54	Luggage rack	16860	$73.00
YF5	California emissions test	4084	$70.00
YJ8	Aluminum wheels	12646	$321.00
ZN1	Towing package	289	$83.00
ZX2	Convenience package	40872	$22.00

quarter of Corvettes sold. Tires were still supplied by Goodyear and Firestone. It is interesting that despite the problems with the latter's Steel Radial 500, they are still shown fitted to the press shot cars for 1977. This was the last year in which the Corvette would carry a full-sized spare.

SUSPENSION & STEERING

Power steering at last became standard equipment for 1977, still using the 'add-on' system first seen on the 1955 Chevrolet. Less than 200 cars had been ordered without it in 1976, and the introduction of radial tires in 1973 and the smaller 14in steering wheel in 1976 meant that driving a '76 without power steering would be hard work indeed.

FE7 Gymkhana suspension continued as before, with heavier front sway bar and springs, and a stiff seven-leaf rear spring in place of the base ten-leaf. As in 1976 the package probably did not include a rear stabilizer bar.

BRAKES

The 1977 master cylinder was a revised design and was distinguished by a shorter pushrod from the booster. All brakes were now power assisted, and the booster was finished in a gold cadmium plate rather than the previous black paint, which was subject to attack from splashed brake fluid.

1978 & 1979

In September 1977 I drove across the USA from coast to coast, the majority of the trip on a drive-away, delivering a 460cu in Mercury Marquess Brougham from Georgia to Southern California. The gas was cheap, the car luxurious and one of the last truly full-size cars before the downsizing of the late 1970s. The new 1978 Corvette had just been announced, and it was being promoted with a billboard poster campaign showing an exact side view of the new model in dual silver. The car had been changed by adding a fastback wrapover glass back window. It looked great in profile but we never got to see an actual car until we were in Texas.

At a breakfast stop, there parked in front of the restaurant was an all-black 1978, the first I had seen. It was brand new and looked gorgeous. The driver's window was down and the new car smell was overwhelming - this was a car to desire.

I had been the owner of a 1966 Sting Ray for a few years and was wondering as we drove across the country how the marque would survive the absurd 55mph national speed limit, the gas shortages and the

general antipathy to nice cars. But here early on a Texas morning, it all became clear. Someone at the Tech Center had looked at the rather tired Corvette and been inspired to do something great with it. By the use of recent glass-forming technology they had transformed the car, cheaply enough to convince the

A third of all 1978s sold were Silver Anniversary editions. Eight-slot alloy wheels and sport mirrors were required options.

Colors 1978			
Code	**Body**	**Quantity**	**Suggested interior trim**
10	Classic White	4150	Black, Dark Blue, Dark Brown, Light Beige, Oyster , Mahogany, Red
13	Silver	3323	Black, Dark Blue, Mahogany, Red
13/07	Silver Anniversary	15283	Black, Oyster, Red
19	Black	4573	Black, Light Beige, Mahogany, Oyster, Red
19/47	Black/Silver	6502	Silver
26	Light Blue	1960	Dark Blue
52	Yellow	71	Black, Dark Brown, Oyster
59	Light beige	1686	Black, Dark Blue, Dark Brown, Light Beige, Mahogany
72	Red	2074	Black, Light Beige, Oyster, Red
82	Mahogany	2121	Black, Dark Brown, Light beige, Mahogany, Oyster
83	Dark Blue	2084	Dark Blue, Light Beige, Oyster
89	Dark Brown	1991	Dark Brown, Light Beige, Oyster
All steel wheels were Argent Silver.			

Big back window (left) transformed the practicality of the Corvette and ensured another five years of production. With more space available due to a compact spare tire and a higher deck, gas tank capacity (below) was increased from 17 to 24 gallons.

management that the Corvette could survive and was worth further investment, and well enough to prepare the car for the '80s.

The ten years of cut-away 'sugar-scoop' rear window treatment was over. It had been a bold statement that had lost its impact: sensational in 1968 but in danger of becoming a trite waste of space by 1977. Originally, the removable rear window had justified the idea of the glass tight up behind the driver's and passenger's heads, but since 1973, when the window became fixed, the effect had been claustrophobic.

Now we were looking at the evolution of the Shark. By adopting the shape of the '63 Split Window it was transformed into a new and better car. The improvement in convenience was inescapable. The briefcase, shopping or overcoat could now be passed over the seat straight into the rear compartment at the same time as the driver sat down, instead of having to be laboriously forced into the space by tilting the seatback forward before sitting down. A petty consideration? Not when you drive a Corvette every day! Now once again a dog could be carried in the car, or even against all recommendations a baby in a carry-cot. This was not what Zora Arkus-Duntov had in mind, but the broader appeal kept the marque alive when other sports cars were disappearing.

That bright sunny Texas morning I was inspired by what I saw and resolved to start my own Corvette business as soon as I got home. I bought the full-size billboard poster of the Anniversary '78

Fastback rear window (above) made the car look lower and faster. Code B2Z Silver Anniversary (below) wore 18 separate stripes.

Glass roofs (right) were fragile and never fitted well.

All 1978 Corvettes carried Silver Anniversary emblems front and rear, whatever the color or Edition.

COLORS 1979

Code	Body	Quantity	Suggested interior trim
10	Classic White	8629	Black, Dark Blue, Dark Green, Light Beige, Oyster , Red
13	Silver	7331	Black, Dark Blue, Dark Green, Oyster, Red
19	Black	10465	Black, Light Beige, Oyster, Red
28	Light Blue	3203	Black, Dark Blue, Oyster
52	Yellow	2357	Black, Light Beige, Oyster
58	Dark Green	2426	Black, Dark Green, Light Beige, Oyster
59	Light Beige	2951	Black, Dark Blue, Dark Green, Light Beige, Red
72	Red	6707	Black, Light Beige, Oyster, Red
82	Dark Brown	4053	Black, Light Beige, Oyster
83	Dark Blue	2084	Black, Dark Blue, Light Beige, Oyster, Red

All steel wheels were Argent Silver.

DIMENSIONS & WEIGHTS 1978

Length	185.2in
Width	69.2in
Height	47.9in
Wheelbase	98.0in
Max track	
Front	58.7in
Rear	59.4in
Curb weight	3550lb

from an advertisement in *Corvette News* and it still hangs proudly in my shop today.

BODY & BODY TRIM

The front bumper, front fenders and hood of the 1978 were exactly the same as the 1977's. An elaborate new 'Silver Anniversary' emblem adorned the nose, replacing the 1977 crossed flags, while those on the front fenders remained the same.

The doors were externally identical too but were modified internally to accept the new door panels and all-new locking mechanisms. New too were the targa roof panels: they were the same shape externally but had a very effective single front latch which also operated a long rod to fasten the rear of the panel. The weather-strip was revised as well. Below the doors the rocker panel was now finished in semi-matt black with just the upper rib left in natural anodized aluminum.

The taller dash pad required a windshield with a deeper, lower blackout area, so a new screen was fitted, the third design since 1968.

The fastback window demanded a new rear deck panel. The large glass was bonded into this and trimmed with a bright stainless steel molding. The rear window happily never leaks. A new larger-diameter gas flap to go with it, also sporting the new 'Silver Anniversary' emblem, covered a bigger gas tank. The capacity was increased from 17 to 24 US gallons by using the new extra space below the canted back panel, as well as the space freed up by the compact spare wheel.

There were two dramatic 'Duo Tone' options for 1978. The first was the B2Z Silver Anniversary paint. With a Dark Silver lower half and Silver top half, the accent stripes were all stick-on decals, a total of 18 different stickers. Sport mirrors and aluminum wheels were required options. This color scheme was so popular that it accounted for more than a third of production and at 15,283 cars painted it remains the biggest color run of any Corvette year yet.

The next most popular color was the Limited Edition Pace Car Replica. The build quantity was originally intended to be limited to just 300 cars, celebrating the specially prepared car that would pace the Indianapolis 500 in May 1978, but the final build quantity was officially 6502. The models was assigned a special serial number with the eighth digit of the VIN a 9 rather than the 4 of regular production, and demand was incredible. This change to the VIN was an inspired move by Chevrolet, preventing fraud from the outset.

Most obvious were new front and rear spoilers. Both were made of flexible molded polyurethane, essential to achieve an easy fit to the Corvette's somewhat variable body. The front was three-piece, leading to cheaper repair for the inevitable damage, particularly of the road-hugging center section. The rear spoiler was one-piece and included a cut-out for the gas filler door. General Motors claimed that drag was reduced by 15 per cent and fuel economy improved by one half mile per gallon.

Finished in Black over Silver, the Pace Car used 15 separate stickers. Cars were supplied to the dealers with the large 'Official Pace Car' sticker for the door, and the small winged-tire Indianapolis Motor Speedway decal for each rear fender rolled up in the luggage area for optional fitting.

Each dealer was assigned a single Pace Car and they were besieged with orders. Enthusiasts who heard early about the Replicas ordered them with their local dealers at list or at a discount, but when Chevrolet salesmen – who generally seem to be the last people to hear about anything that's going

Not built until the spring of 1978, the Pace Car Replica was the subject of a media-driven speculative frenzy. Thousands languished undriven until their owners finally realized that a Pace Car was still just a Corvette, and that most of its special features were 1979 options.

Sport Mirrors had to be fitted with correctly located bevel gaskets to sit level.

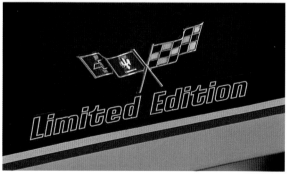

The Pace Car came loaded with options, including tinted laminated glass roofs and polyurethane front and rear spoilers. This decal (right) was applied at St Louis, while the other stickers were supplied packed in the back of the car for the dealer to apply if required by the owner.

of the Wall Street Journal on March 27 1978. Some cars really did change hands for as much as $30,000. The list price was $13,653.21, already much more than the base 1978 at $9,351.89. The race was run and won by Al Unser Jr, who was given Pace Car serial number 90002. Number 900001 was kept by Chevrolet for display. The original car which actually paced the race was serial number 400000, with an H instead of the S as seventh digit, indicating that it was a prototype and the first 1978 built.

on – finally realized what was happening some returned deposits, others hiked up the price by thousands, and options on ordered cars were traded for thousands more. Attorneys litigated, grown men wept in front of their womenfolk. Such was the speculative hype that the story made the front page

CHASSIS

The 1978 and 1979 frames were effectively a carryover from the previous three years' design. This was the last chassis that had the twin holes in the gearbox crossmember to permit fitting of a full dual exhaust.

INTERIOR

The makeover that started in 1977 continued for 1978 with a new one-piece dash panel, containing a new speedometer and tachometer housing for the driver and a lockable glove compartment in front of the passenger. The latter was a typically terrible example of GM's penny-pinching attitude. A five cent lock mechanism ensured that the lid would fall open over any bump, do a multiple bounce and then not refasten. Passengers were not impressed: the only control they could touch had fallen apart, was the whole car this badly made? Japanese glove compartment lids didn't fall apart, they must be better built. We know that most of those Z-cars have rusted away now, and the Corvettes are still running great, but quality is perceived in the most inconsequential details. Ten years earlier the 1963-67 Sting Ray had come with an excellent glove box door and lock.

The foam-filled, cardboard-backed, vinyl-faced door panels that had cracked and disappointed for 13 years were at last consigned to history, together with the frail door pulls. The new panels used a corporate GM design door pull and arm rest fixed to the steel inner panel of the door with three stout screws. The lower part of the panel was carpeted to

match the interior and incorporated small document pockets on each door.

These pockets occupied the position on the door where the window winders had been on non-power window cars. Unfortunately, no one told the door panel designer that power windows were still to be a $130 option for 1978 and a $141 option for 1979... Those drivers who thought they would be smart and not pay the General's ransom for this option found their cars delivered with the window winder spindles punched right through the middle

1979 red leather interior (top). Durable new door panel (above) with map pocket arrived in 1979.

1978 seats were similar to 1977 with a choice of cloth inserts. Dash and door panels were new.

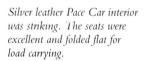

DIMENSIONS & WEIGHTS 1979	
Length	185.2in
Width	69.2in
Height	47.9in
Wheelbase	98.0in
Max track	
Front	58.7in
Rear	59.4in
Curb weight	3480lb

For the first time since 1967, a Corvette with space in the back.

Silver leather Pace Car interior was striking. The seats were excellent and folded flat for load carrying.

of the pockets! Incredibly, this practice continued through 1979.

On cars with the optional cloth seats, this material was also used on the mid part of the door panel. For 1979, the ribbed material was replaced by a houndstooth check.

The door step plates were replaced by an extended carpet finished with inch-wide aluminum strips, and the complex rear quarter retainers at the back of the door opening were gone in favor of a simple fur wind-lace. A matt black molded trim was fitted around the inside of the rear window and a black roller blind pulled out below this to cover the carpeted luggage area.

The 1978 seat belt was at last a single reel design with the spool mechanism mounted high on the B-pillar. Previously, the second reel had been mounted under the seat in a well with no drain, where water from leaking t-roofs accumulated and rusted out the mechanism.

The majority of 1978s were fitted with the 1977 style long-backed seat finished in leather or optionally with cloth center panels. But with the announcement of the Limited Edition Pace Car came an early introduction of the new 1979 lightweight seats, for the Pace Car in Silver leather only. These new seats had no springs but instead used a pair of shaped latex foam cushions, wrapped in leather and vinyl or optionally cloth and leather. The pairs of cushions clipped into a lightweight fiberglass seat which pivoted half way up the back. Both seats were designed to fold flat and were carpeted on the back, and though the steering wheel prevented the driver's seat from folding right down, the facility on the passenger's side allowed quite large loads to be carried. The opportunity was unfortunately missed to make the seats recline, at a time when all the cars competing in the sector offered this simple and essential facility.

INSTRUMENTS & CONTROLS

The new instrument binnacle was a separate unit in the now one-piece dash assembly, and used the same printed circuit technology as the already troublesome five-gauge console, though it is less prone to problems. Both faces were mounted behind a full-width concave plastic lens. The speedometer still read to 140mph with a kilometer subface. A metric speedometer reading to 200kmh and with no mile subface was offered for export. Late in 1979 the first of the new 85mph speedometers were fitted; these would be used through the end of 1982. This was in response to Federal pressure to discourage speeding, giving a frightening insight into the government's mindset and its underestimation of drivers' intelligence. In 1984 the Corvette fought back – the bar graph speedometer still read to 85mph but a second digital unit read to no less than 300mph. The Federal diktat never mentioned a second speedo!

The tachometer for 1978 was redlined at 5300rpm for the L48 and the L82 when fitted with air conditioning. The red line for L82s without refrigeration was 5600rpm. The red lines were the same for 1979, except that air-conditioned L82s were permitted to redline at 5600rpm.

The troublesome combined-function stalk of the 1977 was replaced with a simpler turn signal/headlight dip unit with cruise when this was the chosen option. The wiper switch now went back to the dash, with the option of intermittent wipe if the ZX2 Convenience group was selected.

ENGINES

1978 and 1979 engines are painted blue, and the rule for judging Corvette engines is 'Blue means Boring'. When you open the hood and see a blue block you are not looking at automotive excitement. The painfully underpowered 'sixes of 1953 and '54 cars were painted blue but the first revolutionary 265cu in V8 that saved the Corvette in 1955 and later was a loud orange. Later all the interesting engines – the fuelies, big-blocks and LT1s – were orange too. The dull '75 and '76 motors somehow got painted the same, but for 1977 it was back to blue and it stayed that way through the mid-1982 when, perhaps realizing that the new Cross-fire was actually quite a powerful engine, the blue was banished and, as they say in the fashion world, black became the new orange.

Oil leaks from the valve covers had been a constant problem since 1955. To save a machining operation, Ed Cole's development team had chosen to leave the valve cover mating face on the top of the cylinder head as cast and rely on the cork gasket to seal it. Not a moment too soon, or maybe 23 years too late, the cork gasket was replaced by a red RTV sealant, which is effective for the first five to ten years in keeping the oil off the exhaust manifolds. Most mechanics still elect to use a black hard rubber gasket, backed up with sealant when the time comes for replacement.

L48 The base L48 was a straight carryover from the previous year, but it looked much less impressive because the chromed shield that boxed the distributor and protected the radio from ignition interference was gone. It was replaced by a boomerang shaped black plastic shield lined with metal foil to achieve the same shielding effect for a fraction of the cost. It was also easier to remove for routine servicing, because it simply pushed into place. The block was still the 'oh-one-oh' 3970010, now in its tenth year of service. The cylinder head was now cast number 462624. This engine was five horsepower up on the previous year at 185hp. The California Emission Certification version of the L48, option YF5, was rated at only 175hp. It used a differently calibrated Quadrajet and a specific distributor. The NA6 High Altitude Emissions version used another specially calibrated carburetor and was also rated at only 175hp. Neither was available with the manual transmission.

IDENTIFICATION **1978**		
Engine block cast numbers		
350cu in	3970010, possibly 376450 and 460703	
Stamped engine number suffixes		
CHW	350 185hp	Rochester 4BC manual
CLM	350 185hp	Rochester 4BC auto
CLR	350 175hp	Rochester 4BC auto, Calif
CLS	350 175hp	Rochester 4BC auto, altitude
CMR	350 220hp	Rochester 4BC manual
CMS	350 220hp	Rochester 4BC auto
CUT	350 185hp	Rochester 4BC auto
Chassis numbers		
1Z87L8S400001 through 1Z87L8S440274		
Pace Car Replica 1Z87L8S900001 through 1Z87L8S906502		
(5th digit indicates engine: L=350 175/185hp, X=350 210hp)		

IDENTIFICATION **1979**		
Engine block cast numbers		
350cu in	3970010, later 14016379	
Stamped engine number suffixes		
ZAA	350 195hp	Rochester 4BC manual
ZAB	350 195hp	Rochester 4BC auto
ZAC	350 195hp	Rochester 4BC auto, Calif
ZAD	350 195hp	Rochester 4BC auto, altitude
ZAF	350 195hp	Rochester 4BC manual
ZAH	350 195hp	Rochester 4BC auto
ZAJ	350 185hp	Rochester 4BC auto, Calif
ZBA	350 225hp	Rochester 4BC manual
ZBB	350 225hp	Rochester 4BC auto
Chassis numbers		
1Z8789S400001 through 1Z8789S453807		
(5th digit indicates engine: 8=350 195hp, 4=350 225hp).		

1978 L82 used dual cold air intakes.

The 1979 L48 was a repeat of the 1978 except that the output was raised to 195hp by adopting the dual-inlet air cleaner of the 1978 L82, described below, and by using a less restrictive exhaust system with 2.5in pipe from the front Y rearward. The intake manifold remained cast iron, cast number 14004376 and later 14014433. These were the last cast iron intakes used on Corvettes. The California and High Altitude cars still had special Rochesters and distributors but were now rated at the same horsepower as the other L48s.

L82 high performance motor The optional L82 was also a repeat of the 1977, but with three significant changes, the first of which must have contributed to the 10hp boost to 220hp. The capacity of the cold air system was doubled by running a second air duct along the right-hand inner fender, requiring the air-conditioning pipe to be re-routed to clear the right-hand flex connector. Perhaps more with an eye to weight saving than gas flow, a new aluminum intake manifold, cast 458520, was used on the L82 in 1978, the first on a Corvette since the demise of the 1972 LT1. The new L82 valve covers were marginally lighter, and were finished in gloss black with the fins machined to a bright finish. It was said at the time that they were cast of magnesium alloy, which could not be left unpainted.

Otherwise, the L82 recipe was the same - bigger valves, a more aggressive camshaft, 9.0:1 compression ratio, forged pistons, selected rods and 4-bolt main bearings. The crank was forged and carried an 8in rather than 6.5in vibration damper.

Another lightweight intake manifold, cast 14007378, was added to the L82 early in 1979 production. This, together with further changes to the exhaust system, boosted power up to 225hp, the highest output for five years and more importantly a sign that there was life after the catalytic converter.

COOLING SYSTEM

While the cooling system was a continuation of the previous year's for both 1978 motors and the 1979 L48 base, the L82 cooling system was modified when air conditioning was fitted. An electric fan with plastic blades was fitted just behind the radiator and the shroud was fitted with a sprung trap door that opened at speed.

ELECTRICS

With the increasingly luxurious 'personal car' specification of the Corvette and an option list that was growing again, the electrical complexity of the car started to grow too.

On all Corvettes made until 1982, the fuses that protect the electrical circuits were in a fuse block on the firewall above and beyond the driver's left foot. The block itself is prone to corrosion in this position. Cartridge fuses were used for the last time in 1978 and replaced by the new blade fuses for 1979, and the new fuse blocks have proved more reliable too.

Starting from the front of the car, Guide Power Beam sealed-beam headlamps were used in both years, but from November 1978 General Electric Halogen inner main beam units were fitted to 1979 model cars. The Corvette had been under-lit for years, due to ill-considered Federal restrictions on headlight candlepower and compulsory sealed beams, at a time when the rest of the world was using safer and brighter separate-bulb halogen technology. Unfortunately, the restricted space in the headlight capsule still makes it hard to fit the best modern 5¾in separate-bulb halogen units.

The optional ZX2 Convenience group now included intermittent windshield wipers, controlled by a dash switch with a rotary time delay adjustment. Other convenience group options continued as for 1977. The radio choice too was as for the previous year, and a Citizens Band radio was

Code	Option	Quantity	Price
1YZ37 B	Base Corvette Sport Coupe	49213	$8647.65
1YZ87	Base Corvette Sport Coupe	40274	$9351.89
Z78	Limited Edition Pace Car Replica	6502	$13653.21
L48	Base 350 185hp motor	34037	$0.00
	Base four-speed wide ratio	4777	$0.00
A31	Power windows	36931	$130.00
AU3	Power door locks	12187	$120.00
B2Z	25th anniversary paint	15283	$399.00
CC1	Removable glass roof panels	972	$349.00
C49	Rear window defogger	30912	$95.00
C60	Air conditioning	37638	$605.00
D35	Sport mirrors	38405	$40.00
FE7	Gymkhana suspension	12590	$41.00
G95	Optional rear axle ratio	382	$15.00
K30	Cruise Master cruise control	31608	$99.00
L82	350-220hp engine	12739	$525.00
M21	Four-speed manual close ratio	3385	$0.00
M38	Turbo Hydra-Matic transmission	38614	$0.00
NA6	High altitude emissions	260	$33.00
N37	Tilt/telescopic steering column	37858	$175.00
QBS	White letter radials 255/60 R15	18296	$216.00
QGR	White letter radials 225/70 R15	26203	$51.00
U58	Stereo AM/FM radio	10189	$286.00
U69	AM/FM radio	2057	$199.00
U75	Power antenna	23069	$49.00
U81	Dual rear speakers	12340	$49.00
UM2	Stereo AM/FM 8-Track	20899	$419.00
UP6	Stereo AM/FM with CB	7138	$638.00
UA1	Heavy Duty Battery	28,243	$18.00
YF5	California emissions test	3405	$75.00

added. This was a fully integrated 40-channel AM/FM unit with a hand-held microphone, and was chosen by 4483 buyers. It used a special tri-band antenna, not fitted to other Corvettes. This was the peak period of CB enthusiasm as hereafter the sales would drop year by year so that in 1985, the last year it was available and the beginning of the cellphone era, just 16 were sold.

TRANSMISSIONS

The automatic Turbo Hydra-Matic 350 transmission was being chosen by 80 per cent of buyers through these two years, and this ultra-reliable unit continued unchanged.

The Warner T-10 manual 'box had replaced the Muncie in January 1974, but according to the parts books the Muncie reappeared in 1978 and early 1979 as a wide-ratio M20 four-speed, though not with the L82 high-performance engine. There is some doubt as to whether it was ever fitted at all - certainly from later in 1979 the Warner T-10 was the only manual transmission used, both as wide-ratio M20 with 2.64:1 first gear and close-ratio M21 with 2.43:1 first.

Differential ratio choice was restricted further in 1978, and worse in 1979 when the 3.08:1 ratio was

OPTIONS 1979

Code	Option	Quantity	Price
1YZ87	Base Corvette Sport Coupe	53807	$10220.23
L48	Base 350 195hp motor	39291	$0.00
	Base four-speed wide ratio	8291	$0.00
A31	Power windows	20631	$141.00
AU3	Power door locks	9054	$131.00
CC1	Removable glass roof panels	14480	$365.00
C49	Rear window defogger	41587	$102.00
C60	Air conditioning	47136	$635.00
D35	Sport mirrors	48211	$45.00
D80	Spoilers, front and rear	6853	$265.00
FE7	Gymkhana suspension	12321	$49.00
G95	Optional rear axle ratio	428	$19.00
K30	Cruise control	34445	$113.00
L82	350 225hp engine	14516	$565.00
M21	Four-speed manual close ratio	4062	$0.00
M38	Turbo Hydra-Matic transmission	41454	$0.00
NA6	High altitude emissions	56	$35.00
N37	Tilt/telescopic steering column	47463	$190.00
N90	Aluminum wheels	33741	$380.00
QBS	White letter radials 255/60 R15	17920	$226.20
QGR	White letter radials 225/70 R15	29603	$55.00
U58	Stereo AM/FM radio	9256	$90.00
U69	AM/FM radio	6523	$0.00
U75	Power antenna	35730	$52.00
U81	Dual rear speakers	37754	$52.00
UM2	Stereo AM/FM 8-track	21435	$228.00
UN3	Stereo AM/FM cassette	12110	$234.00
UP6	Stereo AM/FM with CB	4483	$439.00
UA1	Heavy duty battery	3405	$21.00
YF5	California emissions test	3798	$83.00
ZN1	Towing package	1001	$98.00
ZQ2	Power windows and door locks	28465	$272.00
ZX2	Convenience package	41530	$94.00

1978-79 aluminum wheel was polished, with a black recess and black-edged center cap. The majority of buyers ordered these wheels.

which was even worse. A 3.08:1 ring and pinion will fit straight into the differential case, but even allowing for the then 55mph speed limit the choice of ratios was strange.

WHEELS & TIRES

The base wheel for 1978 was still the Rally wheel with its large center cap and wide stainless steel outer trim ring, but now only four came with each car because a compact spare filled the smaller spare wheel compartment. The spare was a black-painted 15 x 5J with a Goodyear P195/80D15 'temporary use only' tire. The full-size wheel would not fit into the wheel tub and had to be carried inside the car in the event of a flat. The sidewall exhorted 'Max. speed 50 mph' and to go any faster with one of these tires, particularly on the rear axle, is alarming indeed.

The YJ8 8-slot aluminum wheel now accounted for more than 60 per cent of production. The aluminum face had a brushed appearance with a black-painted center well, as in 1976 and 1977. The optional Pace Car wheel was polished, with a painted red stripe on the rim face. The plastic center was unpainted but used the same crossed flags emblem.

Tire choice was restricted to Goodyear, with Firestone presumably dropped from the team after the Radial 500 recall debacle. The standard tire was a P225/70 R15 Goodyear Polysteel Radial Blackwall. There was no whitewall or white stripe option, but instead a solid raised white letter tire with the same name.

For the first time an alternate tire size was offered, and this was also standard on the Z78 Pace Car Replica. It was a white outline letter Goodyear GT Radial P255/60 R15, option QBS, and had the same rolling diameter as the narrower tire. To avoid scuffing the body with the wider tires the body was modified on the production line by removing some of the inside lip at the top of the front fender wheel opening as well as some material at lower rear of the fender opening. Additionally, the parts book listed a different part number for a shorter aluminum rocker molding on 1978 cars with Z78 and cars for both years with QBS, to allow the fatter tires to clear the front of this molding.

SUSPENSION, STEERING & BRAKES

The only change was to the standard rear spring, which for 1978 had nine leaves instead of the ten previously used. The width of the spring was increased to 2.5in. The rear housing of the differential was changed at the same time to accommodate the wider spring. There were no changes to the brakes.

discontinued, leaving a choice of only 3.36, 3.55 or 3.70:1. Most automatics were fitted with 3.55:1 so that on a test drive any modern driver will be frustrated by the apparent lack of a top gear. The L82 four-speed was supplied with the 3.70:1 axle,

1980 & 1981

This afternoon I bought another 1980 Corvette. It is a Yellow four-speed with at least 123,000 miles on it. The odometer reads 23,000, so I'm guessing that it's not 223,000, but it could be. The seats are black Connolly leather which I had recovered the first time I owned this car back in 1995, and they still look good. The engine has some extra chrome, and by the way it runs it obviously has a better cam than stock, maybe with flat-top pistons too. I fitted a full cat-free dual stainless steel exhaust back in 1995 and the power is there all the way from idle to 5500rpm. The Borg-Warner T-10 is the wide ratio and the differential is the tall 3.07:1 in the new for 1980 lightweight aluminum casing.

Tomorrow we'll fit a decent FM/CD player and four new speakers, to replace the FM cassette fitted six years ago. The eight-slot GM alloys have been refinished recently and the car runs 255/60 radials on the front and oversized 275/60s on the back. This car drives really well. The clutch is light, the shift easy and it's stable and relaxed at 80 mph with

the engine running at a little over 3000rpm. The ride is excellent too, because a fiberglass rear spring has been fitted and the suspension is well controlled by Koni shocks all round on their softest setting.

Why am I driving a high-mileage $10,000 Yellow 1980 when I could be in my 1997 C5 or even my restored '63 Split-Window? Sure I want to keep the other two clean, and the January roads are

Shovel nose for 1980 was more streamlined and lighter.

COLORS 1980

Code	Body	Quantity	Suggested interior trim
10	Classic White	7780	Black, Claret, Dark Blue, Doeskin, Oyster, Red
13	Silver	4341	Black, Claret, Dark Blue, Oyster, Red
19	Black	7250	Black, Doeskin, Oyster, Red
28	Dark Blue,	4135	Black, Dark Blue, Doeskin, Oyster, Red
47	Dark Brown	2300	Black, Doeskin, Oyster
52	Yellow	2077	Black, Oyster
58	Dark Green	844	Black, Doeskin, Oyster
59	Frost Beige	3070	Black, Claret, Dark Blue, Doeskin, Red.
76	Dark Claret	3451	Black, Claret, Doeskin, Oyster
83	Red	5714	Black, Doeskin, Oyster, Red

All steel wheels were Argent Silver.

The final body for the C3
Corvette was 3.25in longer
than the first and it was also
about 75lb lighter. It had a
lighter frame, aluminum
differential, thinner window
glass, lighter seats and lighter
wheels than the Corvette of
ten years earlier. The new tail
lost the black bumperettes of
the 1975-79.

1981 model had revised front and rear emblems but was otherwise hard to tell from a 1980. The new low-drag body felt quieter and faster on the road. Integrated rear spoiler was neater and carried new emblem.

wet and salty, but also the 1980 is such fun and so satisfying to drive. I like the rugged simplicity of the car, and after all it's the last Corvette made without an ECM controlling the mixture, the idle speed and the ignition advance. If the idle gets a little high when the engine is warm, a quarter turn with a flat-blade screwdriver puts it right. As my right foot brushes the throttle pedal, I can almost feel the vacuum can and the bob weights working to advance and retard the spark.

From the front, or in the other guy's rear view mirror, the long shovel nose is the very essence of Corvette, and on the road the car really does feel more low drag than any previous model. This bright yellow four-speed turns heads like nothing else. My 14 year old daughter, who must have seen me in and traveled in dozens of different Corvettes, makes a point of telling me on reaching home that this car is the one to keep for her wedding present.

She won't get it. I will sell it soon, of course, because everyone likes a 1980. Tens of thousands are in daily use, slightly modified, easy to keep running, tall-geared, economical and far and way the best looking coupe of the era. With the exception of the California LG4 305, it's the last Corvette without a microprocessor too.

When I first lifted the hood of a 1981, I nearly fell over with shock. For a guy who preferred his Sharks without air conditioning, because it upset the under-hood symmetry, the tangled spaghetti of pipes and cables that enveloped the 1981 motor was offensive. Stricter emission regulations for 1981 meant that we all got a development of the California car, and the 350 was once again available in the Golden State. But the 1981 drove smoother and had more bottom-end torque than the 1980, and showed what a powerful effect the computer was going to have in the future.

BODY & BODY TRIM

The 1978 and 1979 models had been 1975s with a fastback. Now for 1980 it was time for the rest of the body to be updated too. Corporate Average Fuel Economy was an important factor in the design of every General Motors car. Even a tenth of a mile per

COLORS 1981

Code	Body	Quantity	Suggested interior trim
St Louis up to August 1 1981			
06	Mahogany Metallic	1092	Camel, Dark Red
10	White	6387	Black, Charcoal, Camel, Dark Blue, Dark Red, Medium Red, Silver Gray
13	Silver Metallic	2590	Black, Charcoal, Dark Blue ,Medium Red, Silver Gray
19	Black	4712	Black, Charcoal, Camel, Dark Red, Medium Red, Silver Gray
24	Bright Blue Metallic	1	Charcoal, Camel, Dark Blue, Silver Gray
28	Dark Blue Metallic	2522	Camel, Dark Blue, Medium Red, Silver Gray
52	Yellow	1031	Black, Charcoal, Camel
59	Beige	3842	Camel, dark Blue, Dark Red, Medium Red
75	Red	4310	Black, Charcoal, Camel, Medium Red, Silver Gray
79	Maroon Metallic	1,618	Black, Charcoal, Camel, Medium Red, Silver Gray
84	Charcoal Metallic	3485	Black, Charcoal, Camel, Medium Red, Silver Gray
Bowling Green from June 1 1981			
33	Silver Metallic	3369	Charcoal, Dark Blue, Dark Red, Silver Gray
38	Dark Blue Metallic	496	Camel, Dark Blue, Silver Gray
39	Charcoal Metallic	613	Charcoal, Dark Red, Silver Gray
50	Beige	2239	Charcoal, Camel, Dark Blue, Dark Red,
74	Dark Bronze	432	Charcoal, Camel
80	Autumn Red	1505	Charcoal, Camel, Dark Red, Silver Gray
98	Dark Claret Metallic	-	Camel, Dark Red, Silver Gray
33/38	Silver/Dark Blue	-	Dark Blue, Silver Gray
33/39	Silver/Charcoal	-	Dark Blue, Silver Gray
50/74	Beige/Dark Bronze	-	Camel
80/98	Autumn Red/Dark Claret	-	Dark Red, Silver Gray

Dual color quantities are included in their first (upper) color quantity.

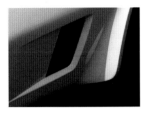

The new nose extended back to the wheel opening. The deep spoiler deflected 40% more air to the radiator and air-conditioning condenser.

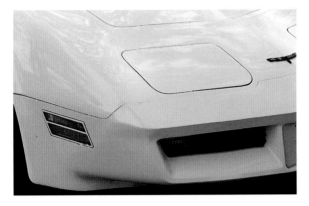

Front fender outlets (above) were now finished with black plastic grilles. 1980-81 cars had no fender emblem except for the 1980 L82. New hood panel (right) was lower and much lighter than previous years. 1981 emblems (below) had black rather than chrome outline.

DIMENSIONS & WEIGHTS 1980	
Length	185.3in
Width	69.2in
Height	48.0in
Wheelbase	98.0in
Max track	
Front	58.7in
Rear	59.4in
Curb weight	3330lb

DIMENSIONS & WEIGHTS 1981	
Length	185.3in
Width	69.2in
Height	48.0in
Wheelbase	98.0in
Max track	
Front	58.7in
Rear	59.4in
Curb weight	3300lb

gallon was eagerly sought and contributed to an improvement in the CAFE rating. Reducing aerodynamic drag was a cheap and effective way of using less fuel and the restyled front end and the rear bumper with integral spoiler each played their part. The published figure for the 1980's coefficient of drag was 0.443 compared to 0.503 for the spoiler-equipped 1979.

A new much larger flexible polyurethane moulding covered a new and much lighter deformable bumper assembly. This incorporated more fibreglass than previously, and used a steel drum vacuum reserve canister in place of the former tubular member which had doubled as a reservoir until this year. Often known as the 'shovel' nose it gave the Shark a front end look in keeping with its nickname. The front fender was reshaped ahead of the axle center line and the flexible molding extended all the way to the front wheel.

The hood panel was lower in profile, and made, along with many other panels such as the door skins and the roof panels, of Sheet Molding Compound (SMC). This was a constant-thickness smooth-finish extruded sandwich sheet, delivered uncured, which was laid into the heated matched die presses to form the body panels. Previously the panels were pressed

using labor intensive 'preforms'. A new wider emblem was used on the nose panel, with a chrome outline for 1980 and black for 1981. There were no side emblems, apart from the fender emblem of the 1980 L82.

A weight reduced rear inner bumper and cushions was hidden by the new tail with the integral 'Kamm theory' spoiler. Both bumper units lost the over-riders of the previous five years. The top face of this rear bumper was alway sprone to rippling.

CHASSIS

It is a matter of pride to Shark owners that their running gear hardly changed over the full 15 years of production - it proves to us how good the design was. The chassis itself ran a full 20 model years. This certainly suited General Motors, who must have recovered their development costs with the Sting Ray before Shark production even began. In the space of 20 years the design went from revolutionary to archaic, with only two minor changes. The first had been the diagonal reinforcing struts linking the kick-ups to the number three crossmember, introduced in 1969.

Now for 1980 the chassis frame was lightened as part of the drastic fuel-saving effort for the new decade. The weight saving on the whole car was about 250lb, and while this was also found in the front bumper and lighter rear axle, a substantial part came from the lighter frame.

Because all cars were now fitted with a single catalytic converter, and had been since 1975, the second crossmember which supported the rear of the transmission was redesigned without the twin exhaust holes. Thus it was no longer possible to order and fit a 1974 dual exhaust if the catalytic converter system was to be replaced 'for off-road use only', as had been possible for the previous five years. This crossmember was as always welded into place if the car had manual transmission, and was detachable on automatics. The new 1980-82 aluminum differential incorporated its own rubber-bushed crossmember integral with the rear cover, replacing the previous heavy steel unit, and this was fixed to new brackets on the main rails.

It is probably true to say that the new lighter frame bent more easily in an accident, particularly at the 'S' curves behind the front wheels, but the other improvements surely outweighed this.

INTERIOR

Seated behind the wheel of the new 1980, it was hard to see many differences from the 1979. Where a cloth interior was specified, a new ribbed material replaced the houndstooth of the previous year. Behind the seats, the center and right-hand compartments were now incorporated into a single

The interior was unchanged from 1979, but power windows and air conditioning were now standard equipment.

1981 had option of driver's power seat for the first time.

unit with a black plastic inner tray concealing the jack and handle. This had been introduced late in 1979 production. The lift hooks were molded plastic too, and broke easily.

Electric windows and air conditioning now became standard equipment. For 1981 the driver's side steel floor was dropped to accommodate a power seat mechanism. For $183.00 the driver's seat was now offered a full range of adjustment to the base, with switches on the front left corner, but the backrest still could not be reclined.

INSTRUMENTS & CONTROLS

Again almost a complete carryover from 1979, the main instrument faces each had a crossed flag emblem to match those on the body. The tachometer had a choke warning light and the 1980 L82 a matching emblem too. Only this tachometer had a 6000 rpm redline, all others being redlined at

1981 door panel. Self-colored armrest/door-pull was also used in other GM cars.

1981 steering wheel had black rather than bright polished spokes. This owner has fitted a 160mph speedometer in place of the 'safety' 85mph original.

Smart new chromed air filter deflected attention from the miserable computer-controlled carburetor that it hid.

All 1981s came with the finned magnesium alloy rocker covers previously reserved for the L82 engine, which was now discontinued.

5300rpm. The speedometer continued with the 85mph face introduced late in 1979.

A new gauge appeared in 1980, initially to replace the clock on cars fitted with a digitally tuned radio, which expressed the time in a 12-hour hh:mm format on their screens. This was an oil temperature gauge, which was has been fitted to all Corvettes ever since. At first received with a mystified yawn, it is now recognized as giving a better guide to true engine temperature and it provides an interesting contrast to the water temperature gauge, which only really shows the temperature around the cylinder heads.

Enthusiasts today wait until the oil temperature gauge is reading over 150°F before revving the engines hard. If only this gauge had been fitted to big-blocks 15 years earlier, how many million dollars worth of original matching-numbers motors would have been saved!

A tilt-telescopic steering column became standard equipment from 1980, and the steering wheel spokes were painted black in place of the previous brushed stainless finish. Sport mirrors became standard in 1980 and optional DG7 electric sport mirrors were offered in 1981, adjusted by a mirror select switch and joystick on the center console.

ENGINES

In general the power of the Corvette engine increased or at least remained the same every year from 1975, the first year of the catalytic converter, and at the time of writing that trend continues. For 1980 and '81 we had the exception – a five horsepower drop back on the 1979. Yet with the lighter weight and more streamlined body the car was still faster, so Rule Two still applies: that from 1975 to today, every year of Corvette has been as fast as or faster than its predecessor. If you are a drag racer you will disagree, but then the pleasure of driving a Corvette fast lasts longer than 14 seconds! And you will know that the 1980-82 aluminum differential was too frail for your sport anyway.

L48 350 190hp The base L48 engine was now fitted with the same silver-painted cast 14014432 aluminum intake manifold as the L82 but was otherwise a carryover, even down to the same block and cylinder head numbers. The evergreen 3970010 cylinder block was retired at the end of 1980 after 12 years of service.

L82 350 230hp The L82 was now in its last year and its rating was boosted to 225hp. Only 5069 were sold so this must be seen as a rare Corvette. It carried new L82 emblems on each front fender.

LG4 305 180hp The base Corvette engine had been at least 5.4 liters for 20 years but, for 1980

IDENTIFICATION 1981

Engine block cast numbers
350cu in   14010207

Stamped engine number suffixes
ZDA   350 190hp   Rochester 4BC manual
ZDB   350 190hp   Rochester 4BC auto, Calif
ZDC   350 190hp   Rochester 4BC manual, Calif
ZDD   350 190hp   Rochester 4BC auto

Chassis numbers
Vehicle Identification Numbers (VIN) 1981
St Louis: 1G1AY8764BS400001 through 1G1AY8764BS431611
Bowling Green: 1G1AY8764BS5100001 through
1G1AY8764B5108995
(9th digit varies and is a check code)

only, the clean-minded legislators of the Pacific coast had to be appeased with a 5.0-liter engine, the 305cu in LG4. This standard passenger car engine option was a $50.00 credit, but the California certification jumped from $83.00 to $250.00.

This LG4 motor was a foretaste of the 1981. Ignition advance, idle speed and mixture were controlled by an Electronic Control Module (ECM) located in front of the battery. Exhaust manifolds were tubular low-grade stainless steel of the same dimensions as the cast iron headers. An oxygen sensor, mounted in the left-hand exhaust downpipe, was the essential component in a closed-loop system which sensed the state of the burned mixture and told the ECM.

L81 350 190hp The 1981 engine was the 350cu in version of the California LG4, called the L81. When it came out we were all terrified. With a computer controlling mixture and timing, we felt excluded and redundant. Had the concept of the tune-up lost its meaning? Clearly there was no turning back, so we bought a Monitor 2000 and plugged into the first 1981 that came in for a service. The Assembly Line Diagnostic Link (ALDL) was a multi-plug hidden under the ashtray. Once this was connected and the car information was programmed in, the tiny green LED screen displayed the new world of engine management. The motor could be seen going into closed loop when the oxygen sensor warmed up, the electronic ignition timing was displayed, torque converter lock-up demanded and much more too. A quick roadside stop to remove various connectors under the hood brought up the appropriate trouble codes - I was completely hooked.

There were no changes in 1980 and '81 to the cooling or emissions systems.

ELECTRICS

The headlamps on the 1980 and '81 were Power Beam outer dip/main unite while the inner high beams were General Electric halogens. Parking and turn signal lamps were a new design with an amber lens and a clear bulb.

First used on 1965 Cadillacs, cornering lamps were fitted to the Corvette for the first time in 1980. Combined in a unit with the side marker and repeater lamp, the cornering lamp shone a continuous white beam to the side of the car when the turn signal lever was operated and the lamps were on.

The rear marker lamps were the same as before but the tail lamps were a new flat-lens design with no bright metal trims, retained by Torx screws.

A new larger alternator, rated to 120 amps, was fitted to provide the extra electrical power for the new equipment.

TRANSMISSIONS

The manual transmission for 1980 was the aluminum-cased four-speed Borg Warner Super T-10, selected by just one eighth of buyers. It was only available in wide ratio, and not available with the L82 or with the California LG4 305. For 1981 it was certified for California.

The automatic for 1980 was once again the three-speed Turbo Hydra-Matic 350, but the following year it was replaced with a new version with torque converter lock-up on second and top gears. Lock-up was controlled by the ECM to prevent the slippage normal in an automatic and thus achieve better fuel economy.

1980-82 rear lamps were all plastic and fitted from outside, simplifying bulb changes.

OPTIONS 1980

Code	Option	Quantity	Price
1YZ87	Base Corvette Sport Coupe	40614	$13140.24
L48	Base 350 190hp motor	32324	$0.00
	Base four-speed wide ratio	5726	$0.00
AU3	Power door locks	32692	$140.00
CC1	Removable glass roof panels	19695	$391.00
C49	Rear window defogger	36589	$109.00
F51	Heavy duty shock absorbers	1695	$35.00
FE7	Gymkhana suspension	12321	$55.00
K30	Cruise control	30821	$123.00
L82	350 230hp engine	5069	$595.00
LG4	305 180hp engine, California	3221	Credit $50.00
M18	Four-speed manual close ratio	4062	$0.00
MV4	Turbo Hydra-Matic transmission	34838	$0.00
N90	Aluminum wheels	34128	$407.00
QGR	White letter radials 225/70 R15	26208	$62.00
QXH	White letter radials 255/60 R15	13140	$426.16
U58	Stereo AM/FM radio	6138	$46.00
U69	AM/FM radio	985	$00.00
U75	Power antenna	32863	$56.00
U81	Dual rear speakers	36350	$52.00
UA1	Heavy duty battery	1337	$22.00
UL5	Radio delete	201	Credit $126.00
UM2	Stereo AM/FM 8-track	15708	$155.00
UN3	Stereo AM/FM cassette	15148	$168.00
UP6	Stereo AM/FM with CB	2434	$391.00
V54	Roof panel carrier	3755	$125.00
YF5	California emissions test	3221	$250.00
ZN1	Towing package	796	$105.00

OPTIONS 1981

Code	Option	Quantity	Price
1YY87	Base Corvette Sport Coupe	40606	$16258.52
AU3	Power door locks	36322	$145.00
A42	Power driver seat	29200	$183.00
CC1	Removable glass roof panels	29095	$414.00
C49	Rear window defogger	36893	$119.00
DG7	Electric sport mirrors	13567	$117.00
D84	Two tone paint	5532	$399.00
F51	Heavy duty shock absorbers	1128	$37.00
FE7	Gymkhana suspension	7803	$57.00
K35	Cruise control	35522	$155.00
MM4	Four-speed manual transmission	5757	$0.00
MX3	Turbo Hydra-Matic transmission	34849	$0.00
N90	Aluminum wheels	36485	$428.00
QGR	White letter radials 225/70 R15	21939	$72.00
QXH	White letter radials 255/60 R15	18004	$491.92
U58	Stereo AM/FM radio	5145	$95.00
U75	Power antenna	32903	$55.00
UL5	Radio delete	315	Credit $118.00
UM4	Stereo AM/FM 8-track	8262	$386.00
UM5	Stereo AM/FM 8-track & CB	792	$712.00
UM6	Stereo AM/FM cassette	22892	$423.00
UN5	Stereo AM/FM cassette & CB	2349	$750.00
V54	Roof panel carrier	3303	$135.00
YF5	California emissions test	4951	$46.00
ZN1	Towing package	916	$110.00

1980-82 N90 aluminum wheels were a revised design. They now had single rather than double reinforcements between each slot, and a bright recess and center cap.

The new aluminum-cased differential was fitted with its own mounting crossmember as part of the rear cover. The new differential was much lighter than the previous iron unit with heavy crossmember that it replaced. For 1980 it was only made in a 3.07 ratio, but there were taller ratios for 1981: 2.87:1 with the automatics and an even taller 2.72 ratio for manual cars. Traditionally, manual cars had been sent out with shorter gearing, numerically higher gears. The exception for 1981 was presumably intended to achieve better emissions and economy, even though it would make pulling away on a hill more difficult.

After 17 years there were changes to the driveshafts and flanges for 1980. The driveshafts were now longer and the automatic cars used smaller universal joints, the same as those already in use in the propshaft on automatics. Manual cars for 1980 and 1981 used the same larger joint as previously, but also in a longer shaft. Whereas since 1963 the outer universal joint had been pressed into a yoke, now it was retained by pressed steel caps and small Torx-head setscrews. In practice these have proved inadequate, and careful checking is required at every service. When the outer end of the driveshaft breaks free, the effect is destructive. Interestingly the same size driveshaft joints that had served so well since 1963 continued to be used through 1996.

WHEELS & TIRES

The 8-slot alloy wheel, unchanged since 1976, was redesigned for the last three years of Shark production. It was lighter, had no black paint on the center and was given a clear protective coating. While almost identical to the earlier wheel, it had a single reinforcing rib behind each of the eight 'spokes', which were slightly tapered. The earlier wheel had a double rib behind each spoke and the edges of these were almost parallel.

SUSPENSION & STEERING

The standard rear spring for 1980 was 2½in wide with nine leaves. The spring on the FE7 Gymkhana suspension was the same size but stiffer, and came with an anti-sway bar. Another Corvette tradition – yes, it really has been 20 years - was first seen on 1981 automatics. This was the new fiberglass reinforced composite rear leaf spring, an idea so successful that it has been used on the front too since 1984.

A mono-leaf design, the composite spring weighed only 8lb in contrast to the 44lb of the nine-leaf steel spring still used on manual transmission and FE7 Gymkhana suspension equipped cars. The improvement in ride was astonishing. Because there was no inter-leaf friction, the spring was also able to move in response to bumps more quickly and effectively. Now available to fit the rear of all 1963-82 Corvettes, these springs have been retro-fitted to thousands of older cars. It is important that they are properly controlled by good shock absorbers. The Delcos fitted at the factory were adequate for the first three years or 30,000 miles, after which the cars tend to wallow and float. Composite spring cars always benefit from a good set of adjustable gas shocks, such as Koni, set initially to their softest position.

1982

B ack in the early 1970s we never thought that the 1982 would look like this. The cove-sided 1956-62 Corvette was produced for seven years and the 1963-67 Sting Ray for just five years. So in September 1967, when the new 1968 Corvette was announced, it seemed likely that the new Shark model would have a production life of maybe only three or four years, particularly because the chassis design was already five years old when the new body was fitted to it.

The late '60s were a time of rapid social and technological change. Man was about to land on the moon, the previously ultra-conservative students had become polarized protesters, race riots were racking the large American cities and teenagers were being drafted into a terrible war far away in south-east Asia. The designers in Detroit were constantly changing the automotive product too. There was glib talk of planned obsolescence, but while the styling was changed annually, the underlying technology was in reality hardly changed at all. The Corvette used just two engine blocks for its base motor for the 40 years up to 1991. It used three different front suspensions, four different front brakes, four different windshields and only four

different manual transmissions, the first three of which were almost interchangeable.

The 1963 Buick Riviera was an icon of GM design at its very best, and it was changed into something different but equally good over the next two seasons. Yet by 1968 the Riviera was an

Rare Silver Green 1982. All 1982s carry Cross Fire Injection emblems on the front fenders.

COLORS

Code	Body	Quantity	Suggested interior trim
10	Classic White	7780	Black, Claret, Dark Blue, Doeskin, Oyster, Red
10	White	2975	Charcoal, Camel, Dark Blue, Dark Red, Silver Green, Silver Gray
13	Silver	711	Charcoal, Dark Blue, Dark Red, Silver Gray
19	Black	2357	Charcoal, Camel, Dark Red, Silver Green, Silver Gray
24	Silver Blue	1124	Charcoal, Camel, Silver Gray
26	Dark Blue	562	Camel, Dark Blue, Silver Gray
31	Bright Blue	567	Charcoal, Camel, Dark Blue, Silver Gray
39	Charcoal	1093	Charcoal, Dark Red, Silver Gray
40	Silver Green		Charcoal, Silver Green
56	Gold	648	Charcoal, Camel
59	Silver Beige Collector	6759	Silver Beige
70	Red	2155	Charcoal, Camel, Dark Red, Silver Gray
99	Dark Claret	853	Camel, Dark Red, Silver Gray
10/13	White/Silver	664	Charcoal, Silver Gray
13/39	Silver/Charcoal	1239	Charcoal, Dark Red, Silver Gray
13/99	Silver/Dark Claret	1301	Dark Red, Silver Gray
24/26	Silver Blue/Dark Blue	1667	Dark Blue, Silver Gray

1982s had a proper fuel-injected engine and a four-speed overdrive TH700R4 automatic transmission. They are truly fast and economical.

DIMENSIONS & WEIGHTS 1982

Length	185.3in
Width	69.2in
Height	48.0in
Wheelbase	98.0in
Max track	
Front	58.7in
Rear	59.4in
Curb weight	3300lb

Two-tone color combinations had first appeared in 1981 to celebrate the advanced paint facility at the new Bowling Green, Kentucky assembly plant.

embarrassing mess (unless you own one of course). This was change for change's sake, but incredibly and happily the Corvette escaped the quest for novelty. No on would have believed back then that the exotic and swoopy-fendered new Corvette of 1968 would still be in production essentially unchanged a full 15 years later.

Spanning three decades, the Corvette developed slowly, accommodating the last mad convulsions of the Muscle Car as well as twin assaults from the Federal government on emissions and crash survival which modified the performance, engine design and shape of the car. Having survived all this, from a low point in 1975 the car recovered a little more

power and performance each year until it reached a final glorious flowering in 1982.

The finest expression of the last C3 Corvette was the beautifully finished, limited production Collector Edition Hatchback, but all 1982s are a pleasure to drive. The combination of a truly fuel-injected engine and the superb new four-speed Turbo Hydra-Matic 700 R4 made this a fast and quiet car in a way that the 1968 never was.

With a fine touch for planning, Chevrolet had installed the engine and transmission from the upcoming 1984 C4 Corvette into the last Shark so that the 1984 would not be too 'all-new' when it was launched. With only five extra horsepower the

The Collector Edition cost $4247 extra but still sold 6759 units. Finish was excellent.

The white lens below the front side marker was the turn lamp, which lit the roadside when lights and turn signal were both switched on.

1984 would be a faster car than the 1982, a difference easily explained by its much lower wind resistance. Running the same engine into a new model design was nothing new. This was the same transition that we saw in 1962, when the last of the cove-sided cars had the new 327 range of motors that would go into the 1963 Sting Rays, and when the 1967 327s were copied into the new 1968. Only the 1997 C5 was an all-new combination.

To make a good four-Corvette collection, it would be hard to beat buying the last model of each series. A 1962, definitely the best finished and most refined of the early solid-axle cars, also had better interior space and the most refined exterior

treatment. A 1967 Sting Ray with a gentle 300hp would be an easy choice for its combination of restrained exterior decoration, wider wheels and best designed interior, but it would be harder to choose between the coupe and the convertible. For the last of the 1968-82 series it would be a pleasure to take a 1982, probably the Collector Edition because it is the most fully equipped and best finished. Choosing a six-speed LT4 1996 would complete the set.

There are too many car series in which the final model is the big disappointment, the car that killed the line. It is one of the many pleasures of being involved in the Corvette world that this has never happened, or at least not yet. Two back seats or a V6 engine would terminate the marque for sure.

1982 was the thirtieth year of Corvette production, and at the time of writing in 2001 dealers are already taking orders for an as yet unannounced Fiftieth Anniversary model. Enthusiasts are confident that it will be the best Corvette yet.

BODY & EXTERNAL TRIM

For the third consecutive year White was once again the most popular color for the regular priced non-Collector car. So over 15 years White became the best-selling color overall, and even more surprisingly Red never made the top of the list. For the C4 cars that followed Red would dominate. The stylists and clay modelers responsible for the 1968-82s extraordinary compound curves would have known that White would show off their handiwork better than any other color. But when

Collector door with leather panels and the best quality carpet ever fitted in a Corvette.

all colors cost the same and there was no fallback standard, it is fascinating that the majority of buyers chose as they did. To see a White 1982 on a dull day is always a pleasure, a straight line reflected in the front fender behind the front wheel is twisted

Silver Green leather interior was supremely inviting.

Collector interior with bronze through silver shades of leather.

into an elongated Z, the shapes come alive - there is no other American car to compare.

The 1982 was identifiable at a glance by its fine Cross Fire Injection emblems on either fender. It also had the best of the dual color combinations. The Collector Edition Hatchback was finished a unique Silver Beige, or gold if you prefer, fully striped, with fade-out panels on the hood and doors, and special cloisonné Collector Edition emblems. This was the first Corvette to cost more than $20,000.

INTERIOR

Leather remained a no-cost option on the 1982, with cloth seats and door center panel trims as an alternative. The driver's power seat option was fitted to nearly 90 per cent of cars for this year

Glove box (right) had been fitted since 1978, but the lock still fell apart on 1982s. Power seat (far right) was optional for 1981 and 1982 only. The steel floor was modified to accommodate the mechanism.

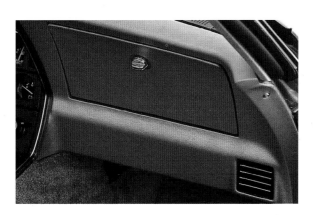

and most are still working well today.

Probably the best of all the interiors from 1968 to 1982 is the Collector Edition's. This version cost $4247.52 more than the base car and a substantial amount of the extra cost went into the interior. Like the 1978 Pace Car with its Silver leather, opinions are polarized about the Silver Beige paint and the adjacent hues of Metallic Brown and Gray that adorn the seats and door panels. Either way, the Collector Edition Hatchback is still the only the only Corvette ever sold with leather-covered door panels and a really good quality carpet. It was also the first with a leather-covered horn push and an opening hatchback.

Hatchbacks bring with them hinges, remote releases, creaks and leaks. Chevrolet scored no more than a pass level on any of these, and all give some problems with higher mileages. Just as the 1963-67 Sting Ray Coupe was spared the problems of hatchbacks because of the costs involved, the 1978-82 fixed back window was always completely troublefree for the same reason. While the hatch on the Collector is a novelty, in reality it is easier to load the stowage area over the folded passenger seat than to lift and stretch over those accentuated fenders. The pull handle and cable release were poor and tended to stiffness and the hinges were insubstantial. Luckily a lesson was learned and the hatchback system fitted to the new 1984 Corvette was superb in every detail, good enough to last unmodified until 1996.

INSTRUMENTS & CONTROLS

Changes to the instruments at this stage of production were never likely to be major, but refinements were still made. The speedometer had always had an odd face since the late-1979 introduction of the 85mph 'safety' upper reading. The logic of this was always suspect - it was about as sensible as the Surgeon General deciding that packets of 20 cigarettes should be marked as containing only ten, assuming that the smoker will smoke only ten and then discard the packet. If this happens, by the way, you'll know that the Surgeon General reads Corvette books!

Previously the speed markings had been in tens ending in five - 35, 45, 55 and so on - but for 1982 all the 5mph increments from 5 to 85 were included. The tachometer was redlined at 5300rpm and was marked 'Cross Fire Injection'.

The analog time clock was still fitted to 1683 cars, but the majority were fitted with an electronically tuned radio with digital clock display, and therefore as before an oil temperature gauge replaced the clock in the five-gauge console. Because the 1982 came with a four-speed automatic transmission the console marking changed to P-R-N-D-3-2-1.

Standard 1982 interior was still luxurious. The 85 mph speedometer has been replaced on this car.

IDENTIFICATION

Engine block cast numbers
350cu in	14010207

Stamped engine number suffixes
ZBA	350 200hp	auto
ZBC	350 200hp	auto, Calif
ZBN	350 200hp	auto, Calif

Chassis numbers
Vehicle Identification Numbers (VIN)
1G1AY8786C5100001 -1G1AY8786C5125408 (6th digit is 0 for the Collector Edition Hatchback, 9th digit varies and is a check code)

Collector Edition included a hatchback (above) with cable-controlled latch. The Computer Command Control system (below) seemed incomprehensible back in 1982, but now we fix them by intuition, experience and back-up from the factory shop manual.

ENGINES

Back in the late 1960s the Chevrolet Camaro Z28 had been raced with a dual-carburetor set-up that was quite different to the compact in-line dual four-barrels fitted to optional engines on the 1956-61 Corvette. On the successfully raced 1967 Camaro Z28 and then on the 1968 and 1969 302cu in production versions a 'cross ram' aluminum intake

manifold was used. This pushed the front Holley carburetor out over the valve cover of cylinders two and four and the rear over five and seven. The front carburetor fed the left-hand bank of combustion chambers and the rear the right-hand bank.

The long intake tracts gave a useful ram effect to boost low- and mid-range torque, and it was apparently to this manifold that the designers initially turned when adapting the Rochester Products Throttle Body Injector (TBI) to the 1982 Corvette and 1982 Z28 Camaro. These injectors were first introduced on the 1980 Cadillac Seville, but their high-profile launch was spoilt by Cadillac's extraordinary decision to make their rough and smelly diesel the standard motor for that year, a panic reaction to the fuel shortages back then. Chevrolet made a much better job of their launch and the smooth and powerful L83 TBI motor was very well received. The new twin injectors worked well on the Chevrolet 350, assisted by yet another cold air induction hood which connected to the open top of the twin-filtered black crackle finished air cleaner. Black crackle paint has adorned the engine components of many Corvette dream cars and experimental cars, but this is the only production Corvette on which it was used.

The camshaft-driven mechanical fuel pump below number two cylinder was now abandoned in

favor of a submerged unit in the tank which was attached to the fuel gauge sender and fuel pick-up. A large in-line filter, the same as the one soon to be used on the 1984, was positioned ahead of the passenger's footwell. The cast 462624 cylinder head continued as before but was now providing a 9.0:1 compression ratio with the higher-compression pistons allowed by the more sophisticated ECM, which updated engine parameters 80 times per second. Torque of the L83 was a healthy 285lb ft at 2800rpm.

Valve covers and other ancillaries were as before, and the engine was now painted black. The tubular exhaust manifolds were similar to the 1981's but now terminated in a 2.5in outlet to a matching front exhaust system and a new low-restriction catalytic converter. There were no changes to the cooling or electrical systems.

TRANSMISSION

The Turbo Hydra-Matic 350 was gone, replaced by the superior TH700 R4 which included an overdrive top gear and a computer-controlled locking torque converter. Third gear was direct and fourth gave an 0.7:1 overdrive, equivalent to a super-tall 36mph per 1000rpm in top gear. Long-distance cruising with a small-block has always been more comfortable with the motor running at 3000rpm or less, and as 3000rpm now gave 108mph it could be truly claimed that the Corvette was a long-legged distance machine. Happily this transmission can be fairly easily and unobtrusively retrofitted to earlier cars too, with driver-operated switching to replace the ECM-controlled functions.

There were no optional axle ratios for the all-aluminum differential, but there were alternatives triggered by, of all things, the wheel choice. The few cars with steel wheels were fitted with the code OA 2.72:1 ratio, other cars with the two types of aluminum wheels used code OF 2.87:1 ratio. While the alloys were the lighter wheels, they were fitted to cars with more options - 'loaded' to use the dealer's favorite phrase - and these presumably required the shorter gearing to retain their top gear performance.

WHEELS & TIRES

Until the 1999 model year, the 1982 Corvette was the only model for which three different wheels were available. Less than 10 per cent of buyers opted to take the base Rally wheel, the rest of non-Collector buyers willingly paying the extra $458 for the N90 eight-slot alloys. For 1982 these had a new emblem on the chromed plastic center cap with the 1982-style crossed flags.

The Collector wheel was closely patterned on a wheel from the other end of the era, the 1967 N89.

It was aluminum and had 36 radial fins. The wheel was finished in a Silver Beige similar to the body color, with the fins clear coated and polished. Just like the 1967, the plastic starburst cover clipped over, with fins intersecting in the same way to cover the hub and chrome-plated wheel nuts. All 1963-67 Sting Rays had come with a matching spare when optional wheels were fitted, but 1982s used the same 15x5 'temporary use only' compact spare as had been fitted since 1978, so only four road wheels were supplied.

The 200hp Cross Fire Injection 350 delivered plenty of low-end torque and used a cold air hood.

1982 N90 aluminum wheel (right). The Rally wheel was still the standard fitting. Collector Edition wheel (far right) was a homage to the 1967 bolt-on alloy wheel. Tire is original.

Options

Code	Option	Quantity	Price
1YY87	Base Corvette Sport Coupe	18648	$18290.07
1YY07	Collector Edition Hatchback	6759	$22537.59
AG9	Power driver seat	22585	$197.00
AU3	Power door locks	23936	$155.00
CC1	Removable glass roof panels	14763	$443.00
C49	Rear window defogger	16886	$129.00
DG7	Electric sport mirrors	20301	$125.00
D84	Two tone paint	4871	$428.00
FE7	Gymkhana suspension	5457	$61.00
K35	Cruise control	24313	$165.00
N90	Aluminum wheels	16884	$458.00
QGR	White letter radials 225/70 R15	5932	$80.00
QXH	White letter radials 255/60 R15	19070	$542.52
U58	Stereo AM/FM radio	1533	$101.00
U75	Power antenna	15557	$60.00
UL5	Radio delete	150	Credit $124.00
UM4	Stereo AM/FM 8-track	923	$386.00
UM6	Stereo AM/FM cassette	20355	$423.00
UN5	Stereo AM/FM cassette & CB	1987	$755.00
V08	Heavy duty cooling	6006	$57.00
V54	Roof panel carrier	1992	$144.00
YF5	California emissions test	4951	$46.00

Tires were once again supplied by Goodyear and the base tire was a P225/70R 15 blackwall, chosen only by 405 buyers. Tire options were either QGR, which was a Goodyear Polysteel Radial in the same profile with raised solid white letters, or QXH, a P255/60R15 Goodyear Eagle GT with outline white letters. These fashionably fat-looking tires were fitted to 75 per cent of 1982 production despite costing more than the N90 aluminum wheels.

Suspension & Steering

All 1982s were fitted with a black plastic tubular splash shield around the outer end of each rear driveshaft to protect the outer universal joint and inner rear wheel bearing. This would have been a useful addition at any time since 1963, so quite why it appeared only in the final year of 20-year cycle is one of those Shark mysteries. More likely it was a fast response to the corrosion problems of the new-for-1980 outer universal joint flanges and their tiny Torx-headed bolts.

RESTORING A 1977 COUPE

Back in 1989 one of my customers told me that he wanted to replace the fuel pipes and brake lines on his low-mileage four-speed 1977 Corvette. The car had seen limited use for 12 years, but on roads that are heavily salted in winter and in a permanently damp British atmosphere, rust can do a lot of damage. We discussed on the telephone the job of changing these pipes and he soon realized that to do it properly the body had to be removed from the chassis.

Following my advice, he first made a castor-wheeled wooden dolly to receive the body, made a scaffolding gantry to sling his hoist from, and loosened or if they were rusted sheared the eight body mounting bolts. Then he removed the front and rear soft bumper covers and the front inner crash absorption assembly, and disconnected the wiring loom, gearshift, steering column, brake pipes and the rest. A 6in wide sling was then threaded under and around the body in the mid-door position, and a powerful hand-operated chain hoist was connected to the sling. After just a morning's work and with a helper to check and steady, he was able to lift the complete body clear of the chassis, roll the chassis away and then drop the body onto the dolly. Now he saw his rolling chassis as no one had since that day in March 1977 when it had rolled freshly assembled and gleaming into the body drop area at the GM assembly plant on Natural Bridge Road, St Louis and received its Maroon targa-roofed two-door coupe body.

He should have ignored the flaking paint on the chassis, the oily leaks on the gearbox and differential, the surface rust on the trailing arms and the inevitable signs of old crash repairs at the front right fender. All he should have done was replace those fuel and brake lines that run along the chassis rails, fit the body back with the new mounts and bolts he had bought from me, and within a week he would have been driving his precious Corvette again.

But my friend is a perfectionist and he couldn't put that body back on yet. He had to address the problems now revealed, so out came the engine and 'box, and off came all the suspension. He was ready to get on with the restoration - but then the sun came out, he put the job aside and he never drove his Corvette again.

He needed a car. Another classic was quickly bought, all the bits of the 'Vette were pushed into the garage and they sat there as nine years passed. Eventually he decided that he would never get round to doing the job and that I should buy the car and restore it myself, and he finally convinced me in September 1998.

We collected the body, still on its dolly, on a rollback, together with the engine, chassis frame, drive line and suspension. Using the dimensions in the 1977 Shop Manual we measured and checked

Wheels, suspension and steering await restoration.

the frame and sent it, together with all the suspension components, straight to the sandblasters to get the restoration underway immediately.

The electro-plater's van calls at our workshop every Friday. We are lucky to be close to one of the country's best chrome platers. Experts know that there is virtually no chrome plating on a 1977 Corvette, but it is their zinc plating service that interests us for the newer cars. Later that day we separated out all the bolts, washers, small brackets, sleeves and spacers, logged them by hand onto sheets of lined paper with a short description, and sent them off for stripping and zinc plating. Some would be missing, but we have saved every bolt we can for 30 years and after plating they are filed by thread size in shallow drawer cabinets, and we are confident that we can always find what we need. To be correct, many brackets, bolts and fittings should be left unpainted. We believe however that

1977 body on dolly, ready for the body shop.

Blue engine paint still just shows on the 1977 L48. When stripped it was found to be perfect inside.

Front suspension is installed on restored chassis.

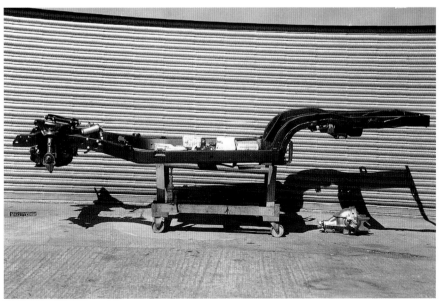

because Corvettes have glassfiber bodies they can be enjoyed in all weathers, so we make sure that our restorations can resist the saltiest winter roads and the dampest British garages.

Every restoration is different. Ideally a car should never be restored. If properly looked after, and if serviced and maintained in accordance with the shop manual, then it should run for ever. However in the real world daily use takes its toll, servicing and cleaning get forgotten, cheap repairs and shortcuts abound, and insurance companies make body shops cut corners on repairs. This car arrived in pieces, so we had no choice but to restore.

In a perfect world a restoration project arrives as a running car, so that every part can be checked, recorded, logged and bagged. Notes can be made and pictures taken of markings, original labels and finishes. We took digital pictures of progress and put them on our website so that the owner and

other interested enthusiasts could monitor progress.

The chassis and suspension were ready a week later, all painted within hours of blasting with a self etching primer followed by a super durable semi-matt black 2-pack. As soon as we had collected the chassis we re-checked its dimensions and then sprayed it internally with a preservative wax.

Once the seats and interior trim had been removed the body was sent off on its dolly to the body and paint shop. The frame was checked again for alignment now that it was all clean and painted. Then we carefully ran taps through threaded bosses and captive nuts on the chassis to clear out paint and old rust and ensure smooth rebuilding. Chevrolet made the car easy to build on the production line by providing all these, so a Corvette is assembled with hundred of bolts – and hardly any nuts.

Now we were able to get on with building the suspension onto the chassis. We used new GM bushes throughout to ensure that the suspension worked as intended while still giving that new car feel. No polyurethane bushes here! Every nut and bolt was zinc plated, so we were able to put them back as matched sets just as they came out. Completely original? No, not quite. Chevrolet saved money on the Corvette by using cheap passenger car shock absorbers that work only on the rebound. Not really a problem on smooth American highways, but on our undulating roads a set of four Koni Classics, set to their soft adjustment, worked wonders to control the big 15x8 eight-slot alloy wheels. Even more important, we fitted a modern fiberglass rear transverse spring in place of the original unyielding nine-leaf steel. Because these have no internal resistance, good double-acting shocks are needed.

When we stripped the original 5.7-liter L48 base engine, code CKZ, which had only 45,000 miles, it proved to be perfect inside because before storing it ten years earlier the last owner had sensibly filled the bores with fresh engine oil through the spark plug holes. We completely rebuilt the engine with new +0.020 bearings on the reground crank, and new piston rings, seals and gaskets. The engine was resprayed the correct (and new for 1977) Chevrolet blue. The original cam was re-used with new lifters. New oil, water and fuel pumps were fitted along with a new air-conditioning compressor. The AIR pump and brackets had been long removed and were not reinstalled. The starter motor and alternator were rebuilt by the local specialist and we rebuilt the HEI distributor. The Quadrajet carburetor was dismantled and put back together with a new seal kit. If it had been worn we would have had it remanufactured by a specialist.

A new clutch assembly was fitted to the refaced flywheel. The Borg-Warner super T-10 gearbox was stripped by our specialist, who returned the cases to us for cleaning and detailing. We then gave them back to him to be rebuilt with new synchromesh rings and a full small parts kit which included all the rollers, retainers, clips, springs and seals. He stripped the 3.36:1 ratio differential at the same time, sent it back to us for cleaning and painting and then rebuilt it with new bearings and seals. The T-10 was then bolted on to the bellhousing and carefully dropped back onto the chassis with new motor mounts. New brake and fuel lines were finally fitted, the same parts that had caused the body-off all those years previously. We did not use stainless steel for these because previous experience has taught that this material is too hard to make a good seal at the flares; instead we used plated Bundy-Weld tubing.

For correctness the exhaust front Y-pipe, catalytic converter and rear Y-pipe should have been installed. However, we took advantage of more liberal British regulations, which do not require a catalytic converter on pre-1992 cars, and fitted a full stainless steel 2in dual exhaust system based on the 1974 design. This fits models through 1979 which retain the two exhaust pipe holes in the transmission crossmember. Stainless steel exhaust systems generally come with a lifetime warranty, so the car can be enjoyed in any weather. The maximum 50 points lost in NCRS Flight judging due to such a system on a 1977 could be regained by driving the car just 110 miles to the Meet. If the entire emissions system was absent a rather longer route of 335 miles would be needed to gain the maximum points equivalent to a perfect original exhaust, catalytic converter and AIR emission system.

While the body was being stripped and prepared by the body shop we were able to prepare the interior. Corvette carpet since 1965 has been heat formed in a press, the shape being retained by a layer of hot-melt material on the back of the carpet. This was ordered from a major Corvette parts supplier, as well as new door panels with the lower carpet and all the trim already attached - expensive but worth it. Most of the other interior trim was repainted with Buckskin dye.

At this point we were offered another very original 1977 with a very poor Buckskin interior. This yielded many original parts for the completion of our project, from air cleaner, fan and fan clutch to radio and rear view mirror, and we then re-equipped it with other useable parts from our car, such as the old door panels, carpets, aluminum flex fan and 14in chrome air cleaner.

Our upholsterer made new leather seats using the covers of the old seats as patterns. We provided him with new seat foams and these were then fitted to the restored frames. At the same time he made a second set of covers to use with the old foams for the other 1977, which we then sold in much improved condition, and for a profit, as a daily

driver! The seat belt webbing was badly stained, but we wanted to keep the belts original, complete with their original labels. So they were soaked overnight in domestic washing machine concentrate and water, then washed again in dishwashing liquid, and they came up like new.

If the body had needed any major new panels, such as a top hood surround panel, then we would have had to do an intermediate body drop. The restored frame would have been wrapped in cling film to protect it from the dust, bonding material and paint. Then the frame would help to locate the panels precisely. We did not need to do this, so the body was completely painted without the chassis in place, just as at it was at St Louis.

The best and the worst rebuild moment is the body drop. Best because the car is once again complete, and worst because you get to love the sight of the Corvette rolling chassis. All your careful

Completed chassis rolls on slave wheels. Fiberglass rear spring was used for a better ride.

Front of rolling chassis showing the massive crash bumper assembly.

work is displayed on that beautiful strong frame and that tough looking driveline, with the contrasting finishes on the plated metal parts and even the frame number clearly showing on the top of the frame rails. Many enthusiasts leave the frame on display for years because they just can't bear to cover it up.

While a single sling had been acceptable for the backyard body lift ten years earlier, more care was needed for the drop. We use two pairs of padded hooks in the wheel arches, just as they did at St Louis, suspended from cross bars which are adjustable for the three different generations of Corvettes with removable bodies – 1984 and later models are of uni-body construction. Each crossbar is lifted at its center by a chain hoist. Perhaps surprisingly, the hooks cause no damage to the newly painted arches. The traditional backyard method for refitting the body is to invite seven buddies round and encourage them with the promise of beer when the body is on. This can work fine but is not recommended. That body is heavier than it looks and it is hard to find safe handholds for everyone to lift. The newer cars are heavier too: this 1977 Coupe weighs 500lb more than a 1963 Coupe and not all the extra is in the chassis.

Once the drop was complete, the body mount bolts were installed and tightened and the long task of reassembly began. The radiator was re-cored, exchange stainless steel brake calipers fitted, the bladder-lined gas tank cleaned out, a new AC Delco battery fitted, and then came a chance to test the rebuilt engine. A big puff of blue smoke and then it settled to a smooth idle and gave off all those great smells that new engines do!

If the car had been older we would have replaced the wiring harnesses completely, but instead we had it checked and repaired as necessary by a qualified electrician. Like most Corvettes it had had a stereo and alarm installed at some time and the wiring from these had to removed. The car was fitted with an ancient Motorola AM/FM cassette which we discarded without a thought. Later, when I showed the finished car to the previous owner, he commented that the car when he had it was nice, but the best thing about it was the very expensive stereo he had installed. Truly, nothing dates faster than car audio!

The final fitting up seemed to take forever compared with the early stages, but then it always does. Even when the tricky installation of the complex bumper system was complete, there were a thousand other jobs to be done. Each task was there to be enjoyed, and as each carefully restored piece was put into place, so the car improved. All the time the carpets, seats and the weather-strip adhesives gave off that great new car smell. The last job, when the car was back to its full weight, was to do a four wheel alignment, dialing in some extra

Radiator support (above) was removed and bolted into body before body was dropped onto chassis. Panels are painted separately (below right), just as at St Louis.

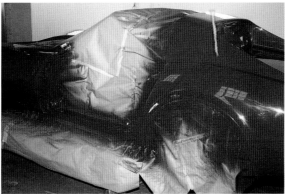

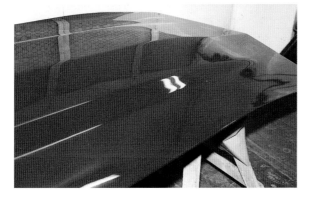

steering castor for improved road feel and high speed stability and to make the most of the wider-profile 255/60 15 BF Goodrich tires.

At last the car was ready for the short drive to the inspection center and a pass of the half-hour test, a call in at the Post Office for the new road tax disc, and then off to have some fun driving it, supported by the essential tool no classic car owner will travel without – a cellphone. This is the best part of all – thrashing round the local bends, and delighting in the new-car feel that follows a proper restoration. I was able to enjoy the smooth torque from the engine, a crisp note from the stainless dual exhaust, a perfect clutch and gearshift, a rattle-free body, and great handling with my preferred extra steering castor settings, Koni shocks and fiberglass rear spring.

The engine noticeably freed up after a few miles, the brakes bedded in and all the time the new interior smelt great. After 30 miles it was time to return to the shop to tighten up and check all the torques, and make final adjustments. Then the car went back to the body shop for a final checkover and polish before being parked in our showroom to sell - and for me to borrow and drive whenever possible!

Restoring cars is an expensive business, but fortunately because of the removable fiberglass body

and separate chassis the Corvette is a comparatively cheap car to work on. Checking the time sheets we spent 600 hours on the car in our workshop, while the body shop charged us for about 200 hours, which included stripping the faded red 1980s paint job and returning the body to its original code 83 Corvette Dark Red.

Installing the interior (above). Everything is available from specialist vendors. Rolled out for the first time (below). The headlight lids need adjusting and the hood with grille is from a 1976.

BIBLIOGRAPHY

There have been an extraordinary number of books about Chevrolet's Corvette, more possibly than about any other car. They vary from the colorful and inaccurate to works of intense research and dry but accurate fact. I have consulted all of those mentioned below, many of which are indispensable to the '68-'82 Corvette owner, and they are listed broadly in order of excellence. Much of the information in this book is gleaned from or checked against these excellent works and their authors and publishers are hereby gratefully acknowledged.

The 'Original Corvette' series is intended to describe and stimulate interest in the history, design and accurate restoration for road use of the Chevrolet Corvette. It cannot pretend or afford to be as deep as is required for a state of the art restoration The restorer is urged to buy at least some of the following, all of which the author considers indispensable.

The NCRS Judging Manuals are highly recommended, and their mail order bookshop can supply all of the following books that are still in print at a members' discount price. Membership is strongly recommended. Write to National Corvette Restorers Society, 6291 Day Road, Cincinnati, Ohio, 45252-1334. Website www.NCRS.org

Ludvigsen, Karl. Corvette - *America's Star Spangled Sports Car*. Automobile Quarterly, Kutztown, Pa. 2nd edition. 1977. ISBN 0-525-08645-5. First published in 1973, this was the first and is still the outstanding narrative work on the Corvette, by an author who worked at GM from 1962 to 1967, and was close to those involved with the development of the 1968.

Ludvigsen, Karl E. editor. *The Best of Corvette News 1957-1976*. Automobile Quarterly, Princeton New Jersey 1976. ISBN 0-915038-07-2. 656 pages of superb articles about the Corvette from Chevrolet's own free magazine. Excellent technical features written without the benefit of hindsight, and full of the flavor of the era.

Various authors. *Corvette Judging Manuals*, 1968-1969, 1970-72, 1973-74, 1975-77, 1978-79, 1980-82. National Corvette Restorers Society, 6291 Day Road, Cincinnati, Ohio, 45252-1334 . Excellent reference and the final arbiter if your Corvette is being NCRS flight judged. The perfect guide to cast and stamped part numbers and original finishes on visible parts for a restored car , based on the widest available information from members of the largest club and constantly updated. The research and dedication of the NCRS members who produced these volumes is outstanding.

Colvin, Alan L. *Chevrolet by the Numbers 1965-69, and 1970-75*. Robert Bentley, Cambridge, Massachusetts 1996. ISBN 0-8376-0956-9 and 0-8376-0927-5. The third and fourth volumes of a four volume series. Fascinating, erudite and correct and beautifully produced, these are outstanding academic works and compulsive reading. As well as the major engine and transmission parts, Colvin covers crankshafts, camshafts and rear axles and much more which is hard to find elsewhere and sensibly concentrates on cast numbers, not the now irrelevant part numbers.

Bizzoco, Rick. *1969 Corvette Stingray Guidebook*. California Trader Publications, Alpine, California 1994. ISBN1-884562-01-9. Intensely researched and exhaustively referenced study of every detail of the 1969. Packed with facts, this is the definitive work on the subject, but not a picture book.

Query, Roy.D. *Corvette an American Legend, Volume 2 1968 - 1986*. Automobile Quarterly, Princeton New Jersey 1987. ISBN 0-915038-51-X. superb color photography of Bloomington Gold-certified cars, with interesting narrative text.

Antonick M.B. *Corvette Restoration - State of the Art*. Michael Bruce Associates. Powell, Ohio,1981. ISBN. 0-933534-14-0. Written with the ace restorer and co-founder of the Bloomington Certification meet Dave Burroughs, this superb book recounts the research and restoration of a 1965 396 convertible. Because the chassis is the same on the 1968-77 models, this book is just as relevant to the newer cars. Burroughs was meticulous in making this car "…the way it was. Not the way we wished it was". This was a very influential book 20 years ago, and it is just as important now.

Antonick M.B. *Corvette Black Book, 1953 – 2000*. Michael Bruce Associates, Powell, Ohio 2000. ISBN 0-933534-46-9. All the information you could need in a pocket-sized format. First published in 1978 and now in its fourteenth edition, and I've got them all! Indispensable.

Amgwert, John. *1968-1982 Corvette Specifications Guide*. National Corvette Restorers Society, Cincinnati Ohio, 2nd Edition 1997. Back pocket sized, this is an essential. Lists the all the important cast numbered and dated components by category, then by year, and much more too. All the Corvette Black Book information and more.

General Motors own *Corvette Shop Manuals* are available for all years 1968-82, though 1968-76 came as two books, Service and Overhaul which confusingly also cover all GM vehicles of those years. Expensive but excellent.

Anonymous. *Assembly Instruction Manual, 1968 to 1982*. Mid America Designs, Effingham, Illinois. Available for most years from 1956 to 1982, these are loose leafed reduced reproductions of the actual drawings sent by Detroit to the assembly plant 500 miles away in St Louis. Parts to build Corvettes arrived at this plant from all over the U.S and Canada, and the A.I.M was the instruction book that the managers had to read to put the car together properly. Dimensions, panel fit gaps, types of bolts and positions of washers and clips, cable and hose routing are all described in detail. Keep it beside you while reassembling your 1968-82.

Lindsay Porter, Tom Falconer, John Pfanstiel and Dave Pollard. *Chevrolet Corvette Purchase and Restoration Guide*. Haynes Publishing, Sparkford, Somerset, UK 1996. ISBN 0 84529 787 1. Based on a complete strip-down and total restoration of a 1969 427 Convertible, this is the perfect illustrated guide for the beginner.

Sloan, Alfred P. Jr. *My Years with General Motors*. Doubleday & Co, New York, 1963. Even if you hated reading this for your high school business studies, it gives a fascinating insight into why General Motors Corporation is what it is, and why the Corvette has survived.

Dobbins, M..F.*Vette Vues Fact Books 1968-1972 and 1973-1977*. Dobbins Restoration Publishing Inc. Hatboro, Pennsylvania, 1991. ISBN 1-880835 00-2 and 0-960-7176-92. These two popular books offer interesting and detailed monochrome pictures of every detail of each year. Informative captions. Excellent coverage of original documentation and labels.

Mueller, Mike. *Sports Car Color History, Corvette 1968-1982* Motorbooks International, Osceola, WI, 2000. ISBN 0-760-30418-1. I have yet to read this one, but everything Mike writes and photographs is excellent, so this will be too.

Licastro,Peter. *Birthplace of Legends*. Just the Facts Publishing, Johnstown,PA 1993. ISBN 0-9630555-8-5. A fascinating history of the St Louis assembly plant illustrated by superb contemporary photographs, many from the St Louis Globe-Democrat collection.

Car and Driver on Corvette 1968-1977. Brooklands Books Ltd, Cobham, UK. 1985. ISBN 0-94648- 9-12. *Car and Driver* was always the best magazine of the era, and this collection of tests and comment is worth buying just for Brock Yates story of his amazing 9000 mile trip in a snow-tired 1976 Corvette from New York to Alaska and back. Inspirational.

INDEX